Generating Creative Images With DALL-E 3

Create accurate images with effective prompting
for real-world applications

Holly Picano

Generating Creative Images With DALL-E 3

Copyright © 2024 Packt Publishing

Group Product Manager: Niranjan Naikwadi

Publishing Product Manager: Nitin Nainani

Book Project Manager: Hemangi Lotlikar

Senior Editor: Shrishti Pandey

Technical Editor: Seemanjay Ameriya

Copy Editor: Safis Editing

Proofreader: Safis Editing

Indexer: Pratik Shirodkar

Production Designer: Vijay Kamble

DevRel Marketing Executive: Vinishka Kalra

First published: March 2024

Production reference: 1220324

Published by Packt Publishing Ltd.

Grosvenor House

11 St Paul's Square

Birmingham

B3 1RB, UK

ISBN 978-1-83508-771-8

www.packtpub.com

To my late mother, whose enduring spirit has been a guiding light. You were with me at the genesis of this book, and as this book comes to fruition, my only wish is that you could be here to see the final product. This dedication stands as a bridge between your unwavering faith and my continuing path. For your love, your encouragement—this is for you. With everlasting love, always.

Holly Picano

Contributors

About the author

Holly Picano stands at the intersection of digital marketing and generative AI. As an expert in both, she's particularly drawn to the capabilities of DALL-E 3, a tool she believes has the power to redefine the industry.

With a Master of Science in digital marketing from Full Sail University, Holly's career has been distinguished by her roles in orchestrating ad campaigns for a roster of high-profile clients, including Hilton and Mayo Clinic. Her academic pursuits have brought her back to Full Sail University, where she serves as an educator, imparting wisdom on the potential of generative AI in marketing.

Holly Picano is a pioneer, continually exploring the frontiers of AI and its applications in creative marketing strategies.

I owe a debt of gratitude to my brother, Mac Autrey. His casual recommendation to explore DALL-E sparked what has become an enduring obsession and the foundation of this book.

About the reviewers

Jasdeep Sidhu is the founder of a generative AI start-up and an independent AI consultant. Previously, he was a machine learning engineer at Workday where he developed an NLP-based fraud detection model. Prior to that, he built an end-to-end data pipeline for 311 service requests as an insight fellow. Jasdeep graduated from the University of Florida with a PhD in computational physics where his work focused on applied machine learning in a distributed computing environment. He completed his BS in engineering physics at the University of California, Berkeley. When not working on AI, he likes to travel, read, hike, and spend time with his family.

Mauricio Sampaio, also known as Mauri Samp, holds a master's degree in multimedia from the Unicamp Institute of Arts and is a product designer from Unesp. In 2000, he was one of the 10 finalists in the Volkswagen Design Competition, and in 2015, he had the same project published in Cartier Art Magazine. In 2023, he had six images generated using AI printed in Figgi magazine. In 2006, he was selected to exhibit at the Eleventh São Paulo Contemporary Art Salon organized by the São Paulo State Department of Culture and held at the Museum of Contemporary Art of the University of São Paulo – MAC-USP. As a 3D modeler, he has a portfolio on Behance.

Greg Downey is the co-founder of the firm AI Tsunami Group LLC and contributor to the book *AI Tsunami: Riding the AI Wave in Business.* Greg was the executive director of the charity The Kelly for Kids Foundation, raising money to provide grants to underprivileged youth. Greg has held leadership positions in marketing, business affairs, broadcasting, and business development at the United States Olympic Committee and NBC Universal, and he was the head of the entertainment division for The Coca-Cola Company. Greg moved to Florida in 2012 to lead NASCAR's brand marketing division and then oversaw the LPGA's strategic partnerships division. He is currently a law professor at Full Sail University.

David Simpson is an emeritus professor of psychology who, for 41 years, taught courses at Carroll University in Waukesha, Wisconsin, USA. During this time, he wrote over 500 blog pieces about his experiences with integrating internet learning tools into the classroom, developed considerable expertise in data analysis and survey development, and was regularly consulted to review books. Since retiring four years ago from active university teaching, he continues to write, learn, and share his learning. In the past two years, he has focused his new learning on developments in AI.

Table of Contents

Part 2: Practical Applications

6

Designing Art for Covers of Books, Magazines, and Other Publications 105

Part 3: The Future of AI and Art

7

Exploring the Ethical Dimensions and the Future of Art 121

8

Effective Prompt Cheat Sheet 135

9

Case Studies, Interviews, and Insights   179

Index   205

Other Books You May Enjoy   212

Preface

Generating Creative Images With DALL-E 3 offers a unique combination of specialized focus, practical guidance, relevance to commercial applications, and ethical awareness. This blend of features sets it apart in the market, making it a valuable resource for anyone looking to explore and master the field of AI-generated art.

Who this book is for

This book is for individuals with interests in art, technology, and creativity. Here are some types of readers who might find this book particularly engaging: artists and designers, educators, and students.

What this book covers

Chapter 1, Introduction to Generative AI and DALL-E 3, explores Generative AI and DALL-E, starting with basic concepts and applications of Generative AI, followed by a practical guide to using DALL-E to create AI-generated art. It combines theory and practice, enabling you to unleash your creativity in crafting unique artwork.

Chapter 2, Your First Creation, teaches you how to create AI-generated art with DALL-E 3, starting with crafting effective textual prompts and generating your first artwork.

Chapter 3, Variations and Fine-Tuning, provides an insightful overview of generating diverse AI art using variations and mastering image attributes and quality through parameters and sizing.

Chapter 4, Crafting Fine Art Prints with DALL-E 3, helps you to master using DALL-E 3 to create fine art prints. You will learn how to convert digital AI art into physical prints with attention to quality and color. This opens up new avenues in the art market by seamlessly blending the digital and physical art worlds.

Chapter 5, DALL-E 3 and the World of NFTs, succinctly covers how to use DALL-E 3 to create and mint AI-generated artwork as NFTs, including an overview of blockchain technology, the minting process, and NFT platforms. It equips you with the knowledge to venture into the NFT art market.

Chapter 6, Designing Art for Covers of Books, Magazines, and Other Publications, provides concise guidance on using DALL-E 3 to create captivating cover art for various publications. It covers conceptualizing, designing, and optimizing art for books, magazine, and specialized publication covers. You will gain skills for producing professional and engaging designs, enhancing your work's impact.

Chapter 7, Exploring the Ethical Dimensions and the Future of Art, briefly explores the ethics of AI in art, covering intellectual property, originality, machine bias, and responsible AI use, while also considering the future of this technology-creativity intersection.

Chapter 8, Effective Prompt Cheat Sheet, offers cheat sheets that serve as an essential starting point for crafting prompts, offering structured templates and examples. By inputting your specific information into these frameworks, you can generate tailored, creative outputs that reflect your individual needs and objectives. These guides are designed to simplify the process, making it easier for you to begin and effectively use prompts for varied and impactful results.

Chapter 9, Case Studies, Interviews, and Insights, encompasses a collection of case studies and interviews with experts across various fields, illustrating the far-reaching impact of AI on different industries. It provides a comprehensive view of how AI is applied and the transformative effects it can have on any sector.

To get the most out of this book

A genuine enthusiasm for creativity and technology will greatly enhance your experience with this book. But rest assured, extensive tech expertise is not a prerequisite to getting started.

Software/platforms you will use in the book	Operating system requirements
DALL-E 3 on OpenAI	Windows or macOS
DALL-E 3 on Bing Creator	Windows or macOS
Canva	Windows or macOS
Fine Art America	Windows or macOS
OpenSea	Windows or macOS
Adobe Photoshop	Windows or macOS

A subscription is required for OpenAI Plus and Adobe Photoshop. All other programs listed have free options available.

Conventions used

There are a number of text conventions used throughout this book.

`Prompts in text`: Indicates prompt words in text. Here is an example: "`Create a coffee mug that says, "TODAY is the BEST day!" make it 1792px by 1024px.`"

Bold: Indicates a new term, an important word, or words that you see onscreen. For instance, words in menus or dialog boxes appear in **bold**. Here is an example: "Microsoft Bing Image Creator offers **Collections**, an area to organize your work."

> **Tips or important notes**
> Appear like this.

Get in touch

Feedback from our readers is always welcome.

General feedback: If you have questions about any aspect of this book, email us at `customercare@packtpub.com` and mention the book title in the subject of your message.

Errata: Although we have taken every care to ensure the accuracy of our content, mistakes do happen. If you have found a mistake in this book, we would be grateful if you would report this to us. Please visit `www.packtpub.com/support/errata` and fill in the form.

Piracy: If you come across any illegal copies of our works in any form on the internet, we would be grateful if you would provide us with the location address or website name. Please contact us at `copyright@packt.com` with a link to the material.

If you are interested in becoming an author: If there is a topic that you have expertise in and you are interested in either writing or contributing to a book, please visit `authors.packtpub.com`.

Share Your Thoughts

Once you've read *Generating Creative Images With DALL-E 3*, we'd love to hear your thoughts! Scan the QR code below to go straight to the Amazon review page for this book and share your feedback.

`https://packt.link/r/1-835-08771-X`

Your review is important to us and the tech community and will help us make sure we're delivering excellent quality content.

Download a free PDF copy of this book

Thanks for purchasing this book!

Do you like to read on the go but are unable to carry your print books everywhere?

Is your eBook purchase not compatible with the device of your choice?

Don't worry, now with every Packt book you get a DRM-free PDF version of that book at no cost.

Read anywhere, any place, on any device. Search, copy, and paste code from your favorite technical books directly into your application.

The perks don't stop there, you can get exclusive access to discounts, newsletters, and great free content in your inbox daily

Follow these simple steps to get the benefits:

1. Scan the QR code or visit the link below

https://packt.link/free-ebook/9781835087718

2. Submit your proof of purchase

3. That's it! We'll send your free PDF and other benefits to your email directly

Part 1:
Getting to Know DALL-E 3

In this part, *Getting to Know DALL-E 3*, serves as an introduction to the revolutionary world of generative AI, with a specific focus on DALL-E. This part explains what generative AI is, how it functions, and why it represents a significant shift in the art and technology landscapes. It digs into the specifics of DALL-E, illustrating its groundbreaking capabilities in image creation from textual descriptions. For both newcomers and those familiar with AI, this part lays the foundation for understanding how DALL-E 3 can be harnessed for creative exploration and artistic innovation.

This part has the following chapters:

- *Chapter 1, Introduction to Generative AI and DALL-E 3*

- *Chapter 2, Your First Creation*

- *Chapter 3, Variations and Fine-Tuning*

1

Introduction to Generative AI and DALL-E 3

In an era marked by the meteoric rise of artificial intelligence, the creative world is undergoing a transformative phase, a renaissance of sorts. *Generating Creative Images With DALL-E 3* is not just a book; it's an odyssey into this new creative frontier. As you leaf through its pages, you'll unravel both the breadth and depth of AI's influence on art, with DALL-E 3 standing at the forefront. From essential concepts to intricate nuances, this book promises a comprehensive guide, catering to both the neophyte eager to dip their toes and the seasoned aficionado looking for deeper dives.

Whether you're an artist aiming to revolutionize your craft, a technophile intrigued by the melding of code and canvas, or simply a curious soul, this book offers a tailored experience. Its modular structure ensures that readers of varying expertise can carve out their unique learning paths by skipping, skimming, or diving deep as they see fit.

But why is this journey essential? As we stand on the cusp of a new age in which AI shapes art, equipping oneself with the know-how isn't just advantageous—it's imperative. By the end of *Generating Creative Images With DALL-E 3* you won't just comprehend the world of AI-generated art; you'll be adept at navigating its waves, harnessing its potential, and creating marvels that speak volumes of the symbiosis between man and machine.

By diving into this first chapter, we lay the groundwork. We introduce the colossal world of AI, demystifying its facets and emphasizing its significance. Here, you'll grasp the distinction between AI and its avant-garde cousin, generative AI. Through real-world examples, we'll elucidate how DALL-E 3, a prodigy in this domain, leverages AI to craft artistry that was once deemed impossible. By the chapter's end, you'll not only fathom the "how" but also the "why," prepping you for the subsequent chapters where theory transforms into practice.

What awaits you in this chapter is a blend of history, tech, and art. We'll explore the following:

- Understanding AI and generative AI

- Exploring how DALL-E 3 uses AI

- Getting started with DALL-E 3

- How to use prompts

- Ethical considerations

Technical requirements

For the average DALL·E user who isn't necessarily diving deep into training the model but rather using it (e.g., via APIs, applications, or platforms that have integrated DALL·E), the technical requirements are significantly reduced and more accessible:

- **Computer or smart device**: A standard computer or laptop.

- **Internet connectivity**: A stable internet connection is necessary.

- **Web browser**: Modern web browsers such as Google Chrome, Mozilla Firefox, Microsoft Edge, or Safari are recommended to ensure compatibility and performance when accessing online platforms that utilize DALL·E.

- **API access** (optional): If you're integrating DALL·E's capabilities into your software or platform, you might need API keys or access credentials. For example, Mixtiles is an emerging photo-centric startup that utilizes innovative software and user-friendly hanging solutions to craft stunning photo walls. By leveraging the DALL·E API, Mixtiles assists users in producing and framing art.

- **Storage**: While you don't need massive amounts of storage to use DALL·E, having some available space is beneficial for saving generated artwork. The default size of a DALL-E 3-generated image is 1024 px x 1024 px.

- **Basic understanding of AI**: While not a "technical" requirement, having a foundational understanding of what AI is and how generative models function can enhance the user experience. In a few chapters, you'll grasp the basics and will become equipped to harness the true potential of DALL-E 3.

It's important to note that for the average user, most of the computational heavy lifting is done on the server side (in the cloud). The user's device simply acts as an interface, sending commands and receiving generated images.

Introduction to AI

Welcome to the fascinating world of **artificial intelligence** (**AI**). As you turn these pages, you are not just reading; you're embarking on a voyage of discovery, uncovering the digital neurons and algorithms that echo the intricacies of the human mind. AI is more than just a technological term; it's the linchpin of the modern digital age, powering innovations that were once mere figments of imagination. This chapter is your key to understanding AI from its roots to its sprawling branches. Why is this understanding crucial? Because AI impacts every facet of our lives, including how we work and interact. By grasping its essence, you will not only be informed but also poised to harness its potential in a myriad of ways.

Understanding AI and generative AI

At its core, AI is about creating machines that can think or act intelligently in ways that traditionally require human intelligence. This can span a broad range of activities, from basic tasks such as sorting data to more complex ones such as driving a car or playing a game of chess.

Generative AI, on the other hand, is a subset of AI that is specifically focused on the creation of content. It's about designing algorithms that can generate new data or content that wasn't in the original training set. For instance, generative AI can be used to produce entirely new images, music, or even text that wasn't explicitly programmed into it. It's "generative" because it creates something new, often leveraging techniques from machine learning models such as **generative adversarial networks** (**GANs**).

In essence, AI is the broader concept of machines being able to carry out tasks smartly, while generative AI is more specialized, honing in on algorithms that can create new content or data from scratch or based on provided datasets.

Let's look at a few examples of AI that you might be familiar with:

- **Virtual assistants**: Tools such as **Siri**, **Alexa**, or **Google Assistant** use AI to understand and process user voice commands to offer answers and perform tasks such as setting reminders and alarms.

- **Recommendation systems**: Platforms such as **Netflix** and **Amazon** use AI algorithms to analyze your behavior and preferences to recommend shows, movies, or products tailored to your tastes.

- **Autonomous vehicles**: Cars equipped with self-driving technology use AI to interpret environmental data from sensors and make driving decisions in real time, adjusting to obstacles, pedestrians, and other vehicles.

Now let's look at a few examples of generative AI:

- **Deepfake videos**: GANs can be used to generate realistic-looking video footage of real people saying or doing things they never did. This technology has the power to create believable "deepfake" videos.

- **Art creation**: Platforms such as DALL-E 3 generate new pieces of art or modify existing ones in distinctive styles inspired by the data they've been trained on.

- **Music composition**: Tools such as OpenAI's **MuseNet** can compose entirely new pieces of music in various styles based on the vast amounts of existing music it has been trained on.

In essence, while all generative AI is AI, not all AI is generative. Having laid the groundwork for an understanding of AI, it's time to pivot to the star of our journey: DALL-E 3. As we transition into the next topic, we'll unravel how DALL-E 3 marries the concepts of generative AI, allowing us to harness its capabilities. Let's dive into the hands-on process of getting started with DALL-E 3 and discover the magic behind it.

Introducing DALL-E 3

DALL-E 3, an evolution in the realm of artificial intelligence, is not merely a tool; it's a canvas awaiting the brushstrokes of curious minds. OpenAI introduced DALL-E in January 2021. The initial idea behind DALL-E was to create an image generation model capable of producing diverse and creative visual outputs based on textual prompts. Its ability to generate unique and often surreal images from textual descriptions sparked significant interest among users, ranging from artists and designers to technology enthusiasts.

They introduced an updated version, DALL-E 2, in April 2022 to create realistic images with high resolution. They went on to introduce DALL-E 3 in September 2023 with the tagline that it *"understands significantly more nuance and detail than our previous systems."* DALL-E 3 possesses the unique capability to transform text prompts into strikingly detailed and sometimes surreal visuals. It blurs the lines between human imagination and machine precision, creating a tapestry of possibilities for artists, designers, and creators.

Exploring how DALL-E 3 uses AI

DALL-E 3 is a remarkable example of the application of generative AI. Developed by OpenAI, DALL-E 3 is specifically an instance of a generative model trained using a variant of the GPT-3 architecture. Here's a step-by-step breakdown of how DALL-E 3 uses AI:

- **Base model**: At its foundation, DALL-E 3 utilizes a version of **GPT-4** (fourth-generation **generative pre-trained transformer**) model. GPT-4 is designed to generate coherent and contextually relevant text over long passages, but its architecture has been modified for DALL-E 3 to produce images instead of text.

- **Training on images and descriptions**: DALL-E 3 has been trained on pairs of natural language descriptions and corresponding images. Over time, it learns the intricate associations between textual descriptions and the vast array of visual features in the images.

- **Transforming text to images**: Once trained, when given a textual prompt (such as "a two-headed flamingo," as seen in *Figure 1.1*), DALL-E 3 leverages its learned associations to generate an image that corresponds to that description. The model essentially paints the description onto a canvas, pixel by pixel:

Figure 1.1: A cubist painting of a two-headed flamingo

- **Generative capability**: The generative power of DALL-E 3 means it can produce not just one but a multitude of images for a given prompt, each with slight variations and interpretations. This showcases its creative capacity.

- **Latent space exploration**: DALL-E 3 operates within a multi-dimensional space called the "**latent space**." Latent space, in one sentence, simply means a representation of compressed data. When it creates images, it's essentially navigating this space to find the right combination of features that match the given prompt.

- **Fine-tuning and constraints**: While DALL-E 3 can generate a wide array of images from a given prompt, users can also fine-tune and constrain its outputs. This might involve guiding the AI to produce images in a particular style or set of parameters.

DALL-E 3 is a testament to the capabilities of generative AI. By learning the intricate relationship between language and visuals, it can imagine and create images from textual descriptions in ways that push the boundaries of machine creativity.

Getting started with DALL-E 3

Starting with DALL-E 3 might seem daunting, given its profound AI background, but in reality, it's elegantly straightforward. At its heart, DALL-E 3 is a generative model driven by textual cues. By understanding how to effectively communicate with this model, anyone can harness its potential.

Using DALL-E 3 requires no deep knowledge of coding or machine learning. It's about guiding an AI, setting parameters, and refining outputs. As you delve deeper into its usage, you'll discover how to craft prompts that elicit the desired response, manipulate image features, and even merge different artistic styles.

This journey with DALL-E 3 is not just about producing images but about learning a new form of collaboration where human creativity meets AI capability. Embrace the process, experiment with prompts, and witness the AI bring your textual vision to visual life. Whether you're aiming to produce digital art or design materials or simply satiate your curiosity, DALL-E 3 stands ready to redefine the limits of what you thought possible.

To begin, navigate to the DALL-E 3 interface on the OpenAI platform: `https://openai.com/dall-e-3`.

Here, after you log in, you'll be met with a simple text box where you can input your descriptive prompts. Think of this box as your command center, where you detail what you envision:

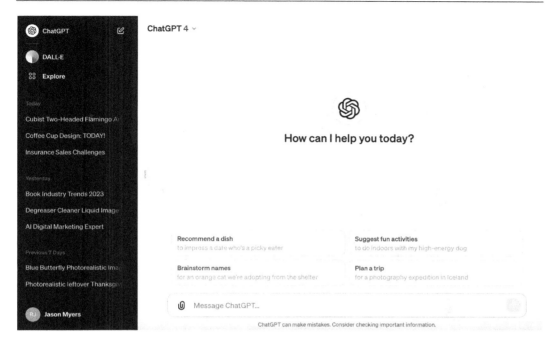

Figure 1.2: DALL-E 3 interface

For instance, inputting "`a two-headed flamingo flying over a rainbow`" will instruct DALL-E 3 to generate an image based on that description. Once you've typed in your prompt, hit the **up arrow** button. In moments, DALL-E 3 will present you with an image that embodies your vision. Remember, specificity helps, and experimentation is key. The more you play around with descriptions and nuances, the better you'll become at harnessing DALL-E's potential for your artistic endeavors.

What you can and cannot create with DALL-E

DALL-E, while groundbreaking, has its realm of expertise and limitations. On the one hand, DALL-E excels at creating vivid and often surreal images from a wide array of descriptive prompts. Whether you're imagining fantastical creatures, blending disparate elements, or conceptualizing futuristic scenes, DALL-E can often bring these to life with surprising detail. It can merge concepts, reimagine objects in various styles, and produce art that feels both novel and familiar. However, DALL-E is not infallible. Its creations are based on its training data, meaning it might sometimes misinterpret or oversimplify complex or ambiguous prompts. Additionally, while DALL-E can generate faces, landscapes, and objects, it may not always produce scientifically accurate or historically precise images. It's crucial to approach DALL-E as a tool for artistic and conceptual exploration rather than an absolute authority on realism or accuracy.

DALL-E, a generative model by OpenAI, offers a wide spectrum of creative possibilities. Here's what you can create with it:

- **Conceptual art**: Provide a unique or abstract description, and DALL-E will generate an artwork that often surpasses the bounds of human imagination.

- **Hybrid creatures**: Merge two or more animals or objects. For example, "a cat with the wings of a butterfly," as seen in *Figure 1.3*, or "a clock-shaped pineapple:"

Figure 1.3: A cat with the wings of a butterfly

- **Reimagined objects**: Ask DALL-E to redesign everyday objects in a specific style or theme, such as "Gothic style laptop" or "steampunk bicycle."

- **Landscapes and sceneries**: From fictional alien terrains to recreations of earthly vistas, DALL-E can generate beautiful landscapes based on your descriptions.

- **Portraits and characters**: Design characters for your stories or games. Descriptions such as "a queen with emerald eyes and silver hair" can come to life.

- **Style transfers**: While not its primary purpose, DALL-E can, to some extent, generate images that mix various artistic styles or themes.

- **Historical or futuristic imagery**: You can task DALL-E with creating images that might resemble past eras or a vision of the future.

- **Abstract concepts**: You can explore abstract ideas, such as "the emotion of joy in a bottle" or "a visual representation of nostalgia."

- **Product designs**: If you're prototyping or conceptualizing a new product, DALL-E can provide visual interpretations of your ideas.

- **Literary visualizations**: Bring scenes or characters from books to visual form, providing illustrative aids for literature.

While DALL-E is powerful, it's essential to remember that its creations depend on the training data it has been exposed to. Some requests might lead to unexpected results, but that's part of the fun and creativity of using such a tool. The more precise and imaginative your prompts, the more intriguing the results can often be!

How to use prompts

Crafting effective prompts for DALL-E is as much an art as it is a science. Prompts guide the AI in generating imagery according to your vision. To begin, you'll start with a concise, clear description of what you envision. For instance, "a two-headed flamingo" or "a skyscraper made of jelly beans." However, the magic often lies in refining and iterating. If DALL-E initially doesn't produce what you have in mind, consider tweaking the prompt for clarity or adding more specific details. Remember to balance specificity with creativity; overly detailed prompts might constrain the AI's imaginative capabilities, while too vague a prompt might yield unexpected results. Experimenting with various phrasings and observing how slight changes can lead to diverse outcomes is key to mastering prompt creation with DALL-E.

Take a look at this example of an initial prompt and an iteration:

Initial prompt: A futuristic cityscape.

The generated image from this might be a generalized representation of a city with tall, sleek buildings, flying cars, and neon lights, as we can see in *Figure 1.4*:

Figure 1.4: A futuristic cityscape

However, let's say you want something more specific:

Iterated prompt: `A futuristic cityscape at sunset with floating gardens and neon billboards.`

This prompt gives results similar to the ones in *Figure 1.5*:

Figure 1.5: A futuristic cityscape with floating gardens and neon billboards

This refined prompt provides DALL-E with more direction, potentially resulting in an image where the setting sun casts a warm glow over towering buildings punctuated by patches of floating greenery and illuminated neon advertisements.

Having unveiled the marvels of DALL-E 3, it's time to dive into one of its most fascinating features: using prompts to shape your creations and the ABCs of DALL-E:

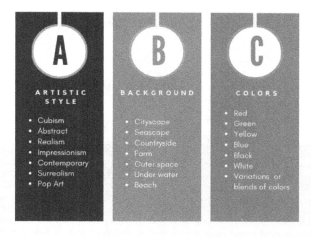

Figure 1.6: ABCs of DALL-E

The "*ABCs of DALL-E*" table is a curated guide designed to optimize the results from DALL-E 3, the neural network known for generating images from textual prompts. While users often have clarity on the object they wish to generate, they occasionally overlook the intricate details that can vastly enhance the final result. Details such as the object's artistic style, the background it's set against, and the palette of colors are crucial for producing a rich and vivid output. The **artistic style, backgrounds, and colors (ABCs)** act as a structured reminder of these essentials. This table not only aids in refining the user's prompt but also emphasizes the balance between machine capability and human artistry. By ensuring each of these aspects is catered to, users can harness the full potential of DALL-E, crafting images that are both technically impressive and aesthetically captivating.

We'll create a few examples to show you how this works.

When we use the simple prompt "dalmatian" in a system such as DALL-E, the system will most likely generate an image of a Dalmatian dog, given that "dalmatian" primarily refers to a breed of dog known for its distinctive black and white or liver-spotted coat. However, without any additional context or descriptors, the exact pose, background, and setting will be determined by the model's training data and its perceived notion of the most typical representation of a Dalmatian. The image might showcase the dog in a generic pose or setting, and there may not be any distinct artistic style, specific background, or unique color patterns beyond the standard appearance of the Dalmatian breed. The output will be based on the model's most common understanding of a "dalmatian" without any specificities:

Figure 1.7: Dalmatian

At the same time, if you input the prompt "dalmatian in pop art style" into DALL-E, the instruction becomes more precise, directing the system towards a specific aesthetic. Instead of a plain representation, the image of the Dalmatian will now encapsulate the vibrant and distinctive characteristics of pop art. You can expect the Dalmatian to be rendered with bright colors, bold outlines, and perhaps repetitive patterns or other hallmarks of the pop art genre. Such a prompt nudges the model to merge the familiar spotted appearance of the Dalmatian with the iconic features of pop art, producing an artwork that blends both the subject and the specified style.

See the example in the following image:

Figure 1.8: Dalmatian in pop art style

Now, we'll try again using more details.

When you enhance the prompt to "`dalmatian in pop art style with pink and blue on the beach`," you're essentially providing DALL-E with a much richer tapestry of details to work from. With this instruction, you're not just asking for a Dalmatian in a pop art style, but you're also specifying a color palette and a setting. The resulting image will likely showcase a Dalmatian that integrates the bold aesthetics of pop art but with dominant shades of pink and blue. These colors might manifest in the Dalmatian's spots, the sky, the water, or even in abstract pop art patterns overlaying the scene. The beach setting might introduce elements such as sand, waves, or even beach props. The blend of the Dalmatian, the pop art style, the specific colors, and the beach backdrop would generate a visually captivating image that combines all these distinct components, offering a unique and tailored visual representation of the given prompt, "`dalmatian in pop art style, with pink and blue on the beach`" (see *Figure 1.9*):

Figure 1.9: Dalmatian in pop art style with pink and blue on the beach

Through this series of images, we observed how we can refine our prompts to match what we envision. Let's look at the takeaways:

- **Prompt specificity**: A generic prompt, such as "`dalmatian`," results in a basic representation. As details are added, such as artistic styles or specific colors, the outcome becomes increasingly aligned with the envisioned result.

- **Artistic integration**: By infusing prompts with descriptors such as "`pop art style`," we saw firsthand how DALL-E interprets and represents varied artistic nuances, blending them seamlessly with the subject.

- **Scene setting**: The inclusion of settings and color schemes, as showcased with "`pink and blue on the beach`," revealed the depth and breadth of DALL-E's capabilities, generating images that are both vivid and contextually relevant.

You have just learned about the intricacies of providing prompts to image-generating systems such as DALL-E. Starting with a basic prompt, such as "`dalmatian`," the system produces a generic representation of the subject. However, by adding specific details, such as "`pop art style`," the image evolves to capture the distinctive characteristics of that art form. Further refining the prompt with additional details, such as specific colors (`pink and blue`) and a setting (`on the beach`), guides the system to create a much more tailored and intricate visual, merging the subject with the specified style, color palette, and environment. Essentially, the more detailed and specific the prompt, the more unique and aligned the generated image will be to the user's vision. Next, we'll walk you through the ethical considerations of AI.

Ethical considerations

While DALL-E is impressively versatile, there are limitations and ethical considerations that restrict its capabilities:

- **Accuracy and reliability**: DALL-E doesn't guarantee accuracy. If you provide a scientific or historically specific description, it might generate an image that looks plausible but isn't accurate or authentic.

- **High-resolution images**: DALL-E, as of the time of writing, mainly generates images at 1024 x 1024 pixels. This resolution might not be suitable for all applications, especially large prints or detailed work.

- **Animation and videos**: DALL-E is designed for static image generation. It doesn't produce animations or videos.

- **Originality guarantee**: While the generated images are often unique, there's no assurance that the model won't produce similar images for different users or prompts.

- **Sensitive content control**: DALL-E might sometimes produce images that some people find inappropriate or offensive, although efforts have been made to mitigate this.

- **Specific art styles**: While DALL-E can mimic a range of styles, it might not perfectly capture the nuances of specific artistic movements or individual artists.

- **Perfect replications**: If you're trying to get DALL-E to replicate a specific existing artwork or image, it won't do it perfectly due to its training on diverse data. This is also a copyright safeguard.

- **Ethical and legal restrictions**: Generating images that infringe on copyrights, portray harmful content, or perpetuate misinformation can be problematic. Users need to be aware of the ethical and legal implications of the images they generate.

- **Context awareness**: DALL-E doesn't "understand" prompts as humans do. It doesn't have a consciousness or real-world awareness, so its creations are solely based on patterns in the data it was trained on.

- **Realistic portraits of non-existent people**: Similar to tools such as **This Person Does Not Exist**, which is an image-generation tool that creates fake photos that resemble the faces of people (these fake portraits look extremely realistic), DALL-E can also create the faces of non-existent people.

Remember, while DALL-E opens doors to vast creative horizons, users should approach its capabilities with an understanding of these limitations and employ the tool responsibly.

Summary

In this chapter, we embarked on a comprehensive journey into the realm of artificial intelligence, with a special focus on generative AI. We uncovered the foundational differences between standard AI and its generative counterpart, illustrating the unique capabilities of each through practical examples. DALL-E's integration of AI principles was demystified, revealing the underlying mechanisms that allow it to craft stunning visuals from mere text prompts.

Furthermore, we delved deep into the practicalities of DALL-E, learning not just its vast capabilities but also its limitations. The art of crafting effective prompts with DALL-E was explored, emphasizing the delicate balance between specificity and creativity. By starting with a simple term, we explored how a basic depiction can evolve into a rich, intricate visual by integrating detailed instructions.

These skills and insights are invaluable because they empower users to harness the full potential of tools such as DALL-E. By understanding the importance of detailed prompts, users can guide the system toward creating images that resonate more profoundly, be it for artistic projects, visual presentations, or other creative endeavors. In essence, mastering prompt specificity allows one to bridge the gap between machine-generated content and human-inspired creativity.

Remember, understanding these nuances is vital as it provides a robust foundation for all the advanced techniques and applications we'll dive into in the subsequent chapters. The insights garnered here not only equip you with the knowledge to leverage DALL-E effectively but also underscore the transformative potential of generative AI in the broader artistic and technological landscape. Armed with this knowledge, you're now better prepared to harness the full potential of AI in your creative endeavors.

In the upcoming chapter, we will embark on a hands-on journey with DALL-E 3.

We'll take the exciting step of creating your very first AI-generated image and go through the process of saving our artistic creations and sharing them with the world. Get ready to transition from understanding the theoretical underpinnings of DALL-E to experiencing its practical magic firsthand!

2
Your First Creation

In the last chapter, we dipped our toes into the world of DALL-E 3. In this chapter, we will be taking a deep dive into the ways of using DALL-E 3. We will cover the process of creating images, making necessary modifications to images, and learning how to save and share the final product.

By the end of this chapter, not only will you be equipped with the knowledge to create with DALL-E 3, but you will also develop an understanding that will allow you to appreciate the harmonious blend of technology and art, a confluence where imagination meets reality.

We're going to cover the following main topics:

- Creating your first DALL-E 3 image
- Modifying your prompt
- Saving and sharing your image

By the end of this chapter, you will know how to craft and modify prompts effectively to create compelling images with DALL-E 3, as well as how to save and share these creations with others.

Technical requirements

As mentioned in the previous chapter, for the average DALL-E 3 user who isn't interested in diving deep into training the model and wants to use it to generate images for varied purposes, the technical requirements are significantly reduced and more accessible. You will need the following:

- **Computer**: A standard computer or laptop.
- **Internet connectivity**: A stable internet connection.
- **Web browser**: Modern web browsers, such as **Google Chrome**, **Mozilla Firefox**, **Microsoft Edge**, or **Safari**, are recommended to ensure compatibility and performance when accessing online platforms that utilize DALL-E 3.

- **API access** (optional): If you want to integrate DALL-E 3's capabilities into your software or platform, you might need API keys or access credentials. For example, **Mixtiles** is an emerging photo-centric start-up that utilizes innovative software and user-friendly hanging solutions to craft stunning photo walls. By leveraging the DALL-E 3 API, Mixtiles assists users in producing and framing art.

- **Storage**: While you don't need massive amounts of storage to use DALL-E 3, having some available space is beneficial for saving generated artwork. The default size of a DALL-E 3 generated image is 1024px x 1024px.

- **Basic understanding of AI**: While not a "technical" requirement, having a foundational understanding of what AI is and how generative models function can enhance the user experience. As we journey into the next chapter, we'll delve deeper into the intricacies of AI. This grounding will allow you to harness the true potential of DALL-E 3, ensuring you get the most out of it.

- **Pricing and subscriptions**: You can access DALL-E 3 through **OpenAI** or **Microsoft Bing Image Creator**:

  - **OpenAI**: `https://openai.com/dall-e-3`

  Accessing DALL-E 3 through OpenAI will cost you $19.99 per month, and this includes a subscription to both ChatGPT and DALL-E 3:

  - **Bing Image Creator**: `https://www.bing.com/images/create`

  You can use Microsoft Bing Image Creator for free as of now. When you start, you're given 15 free "boosts." Boosts speed up the image processing time. Once you use up these free boosts, you can earn more by collecting Microsoft Rewards, or you can purchase them. Just remember, while using Microsoft Bing Image Creator doesn't cost anything, you'll need to pay for additional boosts beyond the initial free ones to get faster image processing.

Now that we're equipped with the necessary technical know-how, let's dive into the exciting process of creating our very first image with DALL-E 3!

Creating your first DALL-E 3 image

Creating an image with DALL-E 3 involves several steps that allow you to transform simple text prompts into vibrant and detailed visual artwork. In the following steps, we will walk through creating an account, getting familiar with the dashboard, generating your very own DALL-E 3 image, how to save your image, and where to find help:

- **Preparation**: You can prepare for using DALL-E 3 by ensuring proper setup with a computer, stable internet, and conducting research for your digital art:

  - **Setup**: All you need is a computer and a stable internet connection.

- **Research**: Before you begin creating your digital art, it is important to refine your concept so you can reverse-engineer your art into your prompts. For example, when I want to create a digital art picture, I will first think about why I am creating it and who my audience is. Then, through this process, I will start to see what prompts will generate the image I am trying to create.

- **Accessing DALL-E 3**: You will be guided on how to access and use DALL-E 3 by navigating to the hosting platform, such as OpenAI or Bing Image Creator, and then signing up or logging into your account to explore its features:

  - **Platform**: Access the platform that provides DALL-E 3 services, such as OpenAI's platform or Microsoft Bing Image Creator. Both utilize DALL-E 3 technology. According to the information available at the time of writing, Bing Image Creator offers free access to image creation. Conversely, OpenAI charges a monthly fee of $19.99. The advantage of OpenAI's platform is that it also features ChatGPT, making it a suitable option for those who need both visual and textual AI outputs. If ChatGPT is not required, the free service provided by Microsoft Bing may be a more cost-effective choice.

  - **Sign-up/Log in**: To use DALL-E 3, either create a new account or log in with an existing one. Refer to *Figure 2.1* for a visual guide to OpenAI's login page. Once logged in, you will be directed to choose DALL-E 3, as depicted in *Figure 2.2*:

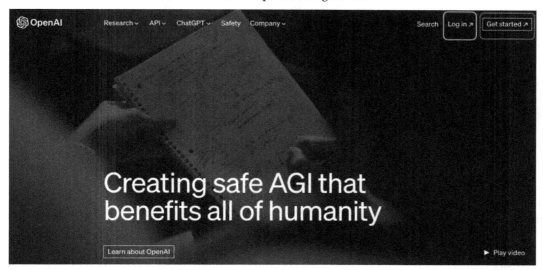

Figure 2.1: OpenAI login page

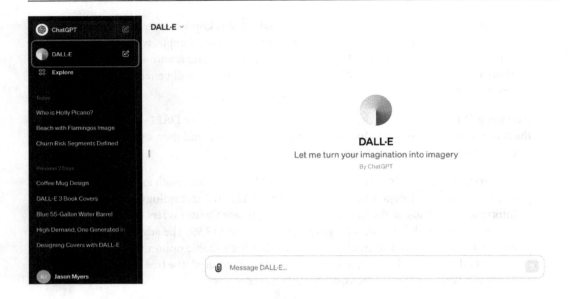

Figure 2.2: Select DALL-E 3 from the options that appear after logging in

- **Understanding the interface**: OpenAI's DALL-E 3 interface is designed to be user-friendly and intuitive, enabling users to generate complex images from textual descriptions. Here's an overview of the typical features and functionalities you might encounter in the DALL-E 3 interface:

  - **Dashboard**: The DALL-E 3 dashboard is straightforward. You simply click on the DALL-E 3 icon located on the left side of the page and type your prompt in the text box.

  - **Help section**: Check out the help or tutorial section at help.openai.com for any guidance on using the platform effectively or for account, login, and billing questions.

- **Creating your art**: You will learn how to effectively use DALL-E 3 by choosing and detailing your prompt with specific descriptions, including selecting an artistic style, background, and color to align with your creative vision:

  - **Choosing a prompt**: Start by selecting a prompt. The prompt is a textual description of the image you wish to create. You will type your prompt into the box shown in *Figure 2.3*:

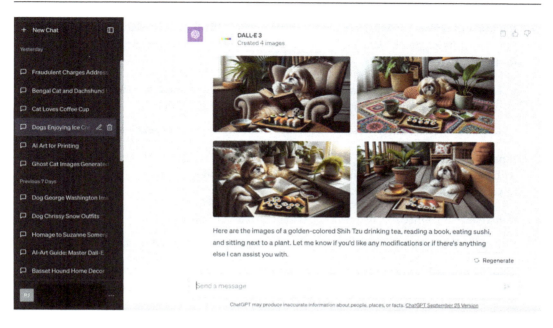

Figure 2.3: DALL-E 3 prompt interface

- **Detailing**: Add details to your prompt. Be as specific as possible to guide DALL-E 3 in creating an image that matches your vision. Use the ABCs of DALL-E 3 covered in the previous chapter by choosing an artistic style, background, and color.

- **Generating the image**: You will learn about executing your detailed prompt in DALL-E 3 and allowing the system at least 20 seconds to process and generate the desired image:

  - **Execution**: Once you have your prompt ready, execute the command to generate the image.

  - **Wait**: When we composed this book, DALL-E 3 typically required about 20 seconds to process a prompt and generate an image. However, as network traffic has increased, the time to create images has been gradually extending.

- **Review and revise**: You will learn about reviewing the initially generated image from DALL-E 3, assessing its alignment with your expectations, and making necessary revisions to the prompt for improved results:

  - **First look**: Once the image is generated, take a look at it and assess whether it matches your expectations. See the *Modifying your prompt* section for more details.

  - **Revisions**: If necessary, tweak your prompt for better results and generate the image again.

- **Finalizing and exporting**: You will learn about finalizing your project by ensuring satisfaction with the DALL-E 3 generated image and then exporting and saving it in your preferred format to your system:

  - **Satisfaction**: Once satisfied with the output, proceed to the next step.

  - **Export**: Export the created image in the desired format and save it to your system.

- **Sharing and utilizing**: You will learn about sharing your DALL-E 3 created images across different platforms and utilizing them in various projects such as digital advertising, graphic design, and NFT creation:

  - **Share**: You can share your creation with others through various platforms.

  - **Utilize**: Utilize your creation in various projects, such as digital advertising, graphic designs, NFTs, and more, by leveraging the powerful capabilities of DALL-E 3.

> **Important note**
>
> DALL-E 3 works best when the prompts are detailed and descriptive, guiding it to create artworks that are as close to your visualization as possible.

Now that you know how to create an image in/using DALL-E 3, let's see how we can generate images using emojis.

Modifying your prompt

In DALL-E 3, while prompts can extend up to a generous limit of 400 words, its extensive training on a dataset encompassing approximately 650 million image and caption pairs equips it to proficiently generate visuals even from concise inputs, including brief phrases or a handful of emojis:

Prompt: 🍕🥤

Figure 2.4: Image result when pizza and wine emojis are entered as a prompt

In the upcoming section, we are going to modify pre-existing image prompts. Modifying your prompt effectively while using DALL-E 3 is a critical step in guiding the AI to generate the specific image you have in mind. As discussed in *Chapter 1*, we started with the basic concept of a Dalmatian dog; in order to refine the image to better match our vision, we enhanced the prompt by incorporating additional details, specifying a "pop art style" (*Figure 1.8*), and further delineating a color scheme of "pink and blue on the beach" (*Figure 1.9*). Through this iterative process, we achieved a depiction that more accurately reflected our intended idea.

Best practices for modifying prompts with DALL-E 3

Now that we know the basics of using DALL-E 3, in this section, we will look at the techniques for using DALL-E 3 effectively, including starting with a base prompt, making incremental adjustments, using descriptive language, specifying orientation, experimenting with artistic styles, choosing the right environment, and iterating based on feedback:

- **Start with a base prompt**: Begin with a simple, clear, and concise description of the image you are envisioning.

- **Incremental adjustments in details**: After observing the initial results, start adding details incrementally to fine-tune the outcome.

- **Use descriptive words**: Use more descriptive words to define the colors, textures, and emotions you want the image to convey. For example, "An eerie, desolate landscape under a muted, stormy sky." or "A whimsical forest with candy-colored trees and a blissful ambiance." These examples encompass a variety of descriptive words.

- **Specify the orientation**: Specify the orientation or perspective, such as "`bird's eye view`" or "`close-up`," to influence the AI's interpretation of the prompt.

- **Experiment with artistic styles**: Experiment with different artistic styles, such as "`surreal`," "`impressionistic`," or "`pop art`," to infuse a distinct artistic approach into the generated image.

- **Environment**: Experiment with different settings and backdrops to set the scene for your image effectively.

- **Iteration**: It's important to follow a feedback loop where you consistently refine the prompt based on the previous outcomes to get closer to the desired result.

- **Research and inspiration**: Before modifying the prompt, seek inspiration from various sources to get a clearer vision of what modifications might work well.

- **Patience and exploration**: Understand that it's a process of trial and error, and being patient during this process is key. Don't hesitate to explore various combinations and permutations of words and phrases in your prompt to see what generates the best results.

After understanding the best practices for modifying prompts with DALL-E 3, let's transition into some concrete examples to better grasp the concept in action.

To solidify our understanding and provide practical insights, let's delve into specific examples of modifying prompts. For our initial example, we'll start with a tranquil forest setting and then adjust the original prompt to achieve varied outcomes.

Initial prompt: A tranquil forest scene.

Figure 2.5: A tranquil forest scene

We see how our prompt leads to generic images of a tranquil forest. Now, let's see how we can make this more specific. Let's say when we think of a tranquil forest, we also envision a babbling brook and morning mist.

Modified prompt: `A tranquil forest scene with a babbling brook and morning mist.`

Figure 2.6: A tranquil forest scene with a babbling brook and morning mist

This prompt is more specific than our initial prompt, but we can make it much more specific. DALL-E 3 boasts an impressive capability to transform images in response to textual prompts, effectively altering visual content by generating specific elements, modifying existing ones, or conceptualizing scenes in entirely new contexts. This AI-driven creative process marries text inputs with image outputs, enabling nuanced image modifications that reflect the intent and imagination behind the prompts, showcasing both the precision and artistic potential of generative AI.

Let's look at the following prompt.

Modified prompt: `A tranquil forest scene with a cottage with smoke coming out of the chimney visible in the distance.`

Figure 2.7: A tranquil forest scene with a cottage with smoke
coming out of the chimney visible in the distance

Amazing! Isn't it? Let's introduce artistic styles as we discussed earlier.

Modified prompt: `A tranquil forest scene portrayed in an impressionistic style with vibrant colors.`

Note

Impressionistic style refers to a 19th-century art movement characterized by small, thin brush strokes, open composition, an emphasis on the accurate depiction of light in its changing qualities (often accentuating the effects of time passage), ordinary subject matter, and unusual visual angles. This style seeks to capture the impression of a moment, especially in terms of the shifting effect of light and color. It was a major departure from the precise and detailed realism that dominated art until that point, leaning more toward a looser, more vivid representation of the subject.

Figure 2.8: A tranquil forest scene portrayed in an impressionistic style with vibrant colors

By iteratively modifying the prompt and being more specific with each modification, you steer DALL-E 3 toward creating an image that is more aligned with your envisioned result.

Now that we've mastered prompt modification, let's delve further into enhancing our outputs by incorporating different elements to modify prompts.

Elements of prompt modification

Let's look at different elements, such as camera angles and positions, lighting, and illustration styles that we can add to our prompts to modify them.

Camera angles

When discussing imagery, film, or photography, a "camera angle" refers to the specific positioning or approach from which the camera captures a subject. Various angles help to convey different emotions, perspectives, and narratives. Here are a few foundational camera angles that are commonly recognized:

Prompt: `[camera angle] of an Australian Shepherd.`

CAMERA ANGLE	EXAMPLES
Extreme close-up This technique emphasizes a small area or detail of the subject, such as eyes, mouth, or a small object.	
Close-up A close-up is a type of shot used in photography and filmmaking that tightly frames a person or an object.	
Medium shot Medium shots offer a balance between showing the subject's facial expressions and body language while also providing some context with the surrounding environment.	

CAMERA ANGLE	EXAMPLES
Long shot Long shots capture a subject within a broad context, usually showing much of the environment around the subject.	
Extreme long shot Extreme long shots capture a vast area, often encompassing expansive landscapes or large-scale sets.	

Table 2.1: Camera angles

Now that we've explored various camera angles, let's shift our focus to understanding different positions and vantage points.

Positions and perspectives

When discussing positions or perspectives, such as "aerial view" or "long angle," in a visual context, we're referring to specific vantage points or orientations from which a subject is depicted or viewed. This concept is crucial in various visual arts, including photography, cinematography, and painting, where various positions can dictate the narrative, aesthetic, and emotional impact of an image. Here are some examples:

Prompt: `[vantage point/perspective]` `of an Australian Shepherd.`

POSITIONS	EXAMPLES
Overhead view An "overhead view" in photography and videography refers to a type of shot that captures a broad, comprehensive view of a scene or subject from above.	
Low angle A low-angle shot is a photographic and cinematic technique where the camera is positioned low on the vertical axis, often at or below the eye level of the subject, and aimed upward.	
Aerial view An aerial view is a perspective seen from an elevated position, often from above the subject, looking down.	
Tilted frame This technique creates a sense of imbalance or disorientation and is used for various artistic and narrative purposes.	

POSITIONS	EXAMPLES
Over-the-shoulder (OTS) An OTS shot is a camera angle used in photography and filmmaking. It is framed from behind a person or animal looking over their shoulder at another subject, typically another character.	

Table 2.2: Positions

Let's now turn our attention to camera settings and lens types.

Camera settings and lenses

Camera settings and lenses play pivotal roles in photography and videography, dictating how a scene is captured, affecting the aesthetics, and enabling various creative possibilities.

CAMERA SETTINGS AND LENSES	EXAMPLES
Slow shutter speed Slow shutter speeds are often used to create a blur effect, showing motion in the image.	
Fast shutter speed Fast shutter speeds are ideal for freezing motion. This makes them perfect for capturing fast-moving subjects, such as in sports photography, wildlife photography, or capturing splashes of water without any blur.	

CAMERA SETTINGS AND LENSES	EXAMPLES
Bokeh Bokeh is a term derived from the Japanese word "boke" (暈け or ボケ), which means "blur" or "haze." In photography, bokeh refers to the aesthetic quality of the blur produced in the out-of-focus parts of an image. This effect is typically seen in areas of an image that lie outside the depth of field.	
Tilt-shift Tilt-shift is popularly used to create a "miniature" effect. By selectively focusing on a small part of the image and blurring the rest (especially in wide, high-angle shots), normal scenes can appear as if they are small-scale models.	
Motion blur Motion blur is a visual effect that occurs when the movement of an object or the camera itself is captured with a slower shutter speed in photography or videography.	
Telephoto lens The primary function of a telephoto lens is to magnify distant subjects, making them appear closer and more prominent in the frame.	

CAMERA SETTINGS AND LENSES	EXAMPLES
Macro lens Macro lenses have a very short minimum focusing distance, allowing photographers to get close to small subjects, such as insects, flowers, and small objects, and still maintain sharp focus.	
Wide-angle lens This allows the lens to capture more of the scene in a single shot.	
Fisheye lens A fisheye lens is a type of ultra-wide-angle lens in photography that produces a distinctive visual distortion intended to create a wide panoramic or hemispherical image.	
Depth of field (DoF) DoF is a term used in photography and cinematography to describe the extent to which the objects in an image are in sharp focus.	

Table 2.3: Camera settings and lenses

We know lighting plays a crucial role in images, so let's move on to examining prompts related to natural and indoor lighting.

Lighting prompts (natural)

Natural lighting, derived from the sun or moon, plays a pivotal role in crafting the aesthetics of visual imagery, as well as shaping the perception, emotion, and depth within a scene. Utilizing natural light can generate various effects, depending on factors such as the time of day, weather, and location:

LIGHTING PROMPTS (NATURAL)	EXAMPLES
Golden hour Golden hour, also known as magic hour, refers to the period of daytime shortly after sunrise or before sunset, during which daylight is redder, softer, and often considered more visually appealing than when the sun is higher in the sky.	
Blue hour Blue hour lighting refers to the unique natural light that occurs during the period of twilight in the morning and evening	
Midday Midday light refers to the natural light that occurs around noon when the sun is at or near its highest point in the sky.	

LIGHTING PROMPTS (NATURAL)	EXAMPLES
Overcast Overcast refers to a weather condition characterized by cloudy skies, where clouds cover most or all of the sky, often resulting in a diffuse, soft light.	
Shadow In the natural world, shadows can reveal the position of the sun or other light sources, and they change in length and direction throughout the day.	
Silhouette Silhouette photography is a popular technique that focuses on the shape and form of the subject rather than its color, texture, or other details.	

Table 2.4: Lighting outdoors

Lighting prompts (indoor)

Indoor lighting brings a nuanced dynamic to visual content, shaping the ambiance, clarity, and overall aesthetic of a scene within enclosed spaces. Different types of indoor lighting create various effects, influences, and moods in imagery:

LIGHTING (INDOOR)	EXAMPLES
Warm lighting Warm lighting refers to the use of light sources that emit a warm or yellowish color temperature. This type of lighting creates a cozy, inviting, and relaxed atmosphere, often associated with comfort and intimacy.	
Cold lighting Cold lighting refers to a type of lighting that has a blue or bluish-white tint, giving a cooler, crisper appearance to the illuminated area or object.	
Flash photography Flash photography refers to the use of a flash device to produce a short burst of artificial light, typically used to illuminate a scene or subject in photography. This technique is particularly useful in low-light conditions or when there's a need to control the lighting of the subject more precisely.	
High-key lighting High-key lighting is a style of lighting used in photography, film, and television characterized by its bright and evenly distributed light. It minimizes shadow and contrast, resulting in a light, airy, and optimistic mood.	

LIGHTING (INDOOR)	EXAMPLES
Low-key lighting Low-key lighting is a cinematic and photographic technique characterized by its use of deep shadows, high contrast, and a predominance of dark tones. This style of lighting creates a moody, dramatic, and often more intimate visual aesthetic.	
Backlighting Backlighting is a photography and cinematography technique where the lighting source is placed behind the subject, pointing toward the camera.	
Studio lighting Studio lighting is commonly used in portrait photography and product photography to achieve flattering and controlled lighting on subjects or products.	
Direction lighting Directional lighting is a lighting technique used in photography, cinematography, and stage lighting where the primary source of light is positioned to come from a specific direction relative to the subject or scene.	

Table 2.5: Lighting indoors

Let's explore different creative film types next.

Creative film types

While DALL-E 3 doesn't process film or comprehend it in the way human photographers do, you can attempt to guide its image generation towards mimicking certain film aesthetics by integrating film-type descriptions into your textual prompts. Here are some examples:

CREATIVE FILM TYPES	EXAMPLES
Kodachrome Kodachrome was a brand of color film introduced by Eastman Kodak in 1935. It became one of the most popular types of color film and was renowned for its rich color accuracy, fine grain, and sharpness.	
Lomography Lomographic images are known for their high contrasts, saturation, and vignettes.	
Polaroid Polaroid refers to a brand of instant film and cameras famous for their ability to produce a developed film image instantly after taking a picture.	

CREATIVE FILM TYPES	EXAMPLES
Closed-circuit television (CCTV) CCTV is a type of video surveillance system used to monitor and record activities in a specific area for security and safety purposes.	
Daguerreotype These images are typically very delicate and exhibit a mirror-like surface. Depending on the angle of view, they can appear as a positive or a negative.	
Double exposure Double exposure is a photographic technique that combines two different images into a single frame.	
Contact sheet A contact sheet is a photographic tool used primarily in film photography, acting as a quick reference and overview of all the negatives from a roll of film.	

CREATIVE FILM TYPES	EXAMPLES
Color splash Color splash is a creative photographic effect where most of a photo is converted to black and white, but some parts are left in color.	

Table 2.6: Creative film types

Let's look at prompts related to various illustration styles next.

Illustration styles

Illustration styles refer to distinctive visual approaches and techniques employed in the creation of illustrative art, each embodying unique attributes, aesthetics, and expressive capabilities. They encapsulate various elements such as line work, color usage, textural qualities, and compositional methodologies, offering a diverse spectrum of visual narratives across different themes and contexts. Here are some examples:

ILLUSTRATION STYLES	EXAMPLES
Pencil sketch A drawing or artwork created using pencils.	

ILLUSTRATION STYLES	EXAMPLES
Pen and ink Pen and ink is a traditional drawing and illustration technique that involves using pens and ink to create artwork, drawings, or illustrations.	
Realistic pencil drawing A realistic pencil drawing is a highly detailed and accurate representation of a subject or scene created using graphite pencils or charcoal pencils.	
Charcoal Charcoal is known for its ability to create deep, dark, and bold lines and shading, making it well suited for achieving strong contrasts in a drawing.	
Wood carving Wood carving is a traditional and versatile form of visual art and craftsmanship that involves the cutting, shaping, and removal of wood to create three-dimensional objects, sculptures, decorative items, or relief carvings.	

ILLUSTRATION STYLES	EXAMPLES
Line art Line art, also known as line drawing, is a style of visual art in which artists use lines, either solid or broken, to create two-dimensional images or illustrations.	
Etching Etching is a printmaking technique in the visual arts in which an image is created on a metal plate using an acid or chemical process.	
Crayon Crayons are a popular medium for children's art activities.	
Children's drawing Children's drawings are typically characterized by their unique and spontaneous style, often reflecting the child's age, developmental stage, and personal creativity.	

ILLUSTRATION STYLES	EXAMPLES
Watercolor Watercolor is known for its transparent and fluid qualities, making it a popular choice among artists for creating colorful and expressive paintings.	
Pastels Pastels consist of pure pigment mixed with a binder to create sticks or crayons of colored material.	
Colored pencil Colored pencils are precise tools that allow for detailed and controlled coloring and drawing.	
Airbrush An airbrush is a versatile and precis painting tool that uses compressed air to spray a fine mist of paint onto a surface. It is commonly used in various artistic, illustrative, and industrial applications to achieve smooth and even color application, gradients, and detailed effects.	

ILLUSTRATION STYLES	EXAMPLES
Ukiyo-e Ukiyo-e, a term literally translating to "pictures of the floating world," is a genre of Japanese art that flourished from the 17th through the 19th centuries. It's primarily known for its woodblock prints and paintings.	
Chinese brushstroke Chinese brushstroke refers to a distinctive style of painting and calligraphy that originated in China and is known for its emphasis on motion, precision, and the spiritual representation of subjects.	
Collage A collage is a form of visual art that involves assembling various materials onto a single surface to create a new, unified composition.	
Screen printing Screen printing, also known as silkscreen or serigraphy, is a printing technique that allows for the transfer of an image onto a substrate (such as paper, fabric, or wood) using a mesh screen, ink, and a squeegee.	

ILLUSTRATION STYLES	EXAMPLES
Sticker illustration Sticker illustration refers to the creation of illustrated images or designs that are intended to be used as digital or physical stickers.	
Layered paper Layered paper refers to the technique of creating three-dimensional artwork by stacking or layering sheets of paper on top of each other.	
Low poly Low poly, short for "low polygon," is a style in computer graphics and 3D modeling that uses a relatively small number of polygons. Polygons, typically triangles or quadrilaterals, are the basic units used in 3D modeling to construct the surfaces of objects.	

Table 2.7: Illustration styles

Illustration styles that are specifically instructional styles

Instructional illustration refers to a visual depiction designed to instruct, guide, or provide information in a clear and effective manner. This specific style of illustration aims to simplify complex information, making it easily digestible and accessible to a wide audience. Here are some examples:

ILLUSTRATION STYLES	EXAMPLES
Blueprint A blueprint is a technical or architectural drawing or plan that outlines the design, dimensions, and specifications of a building, structure, or mechanical system.	
Patent drawing A patent drawing is a visual representation of an invention, design, or process that provides additional clarity and information about the invention being patented.	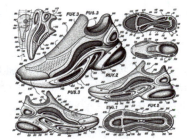
Cutaway The primary purpose of a cutaway is to provide a clear and detailed view of the internal features of an object or structure that would otherwise be hidden from view.	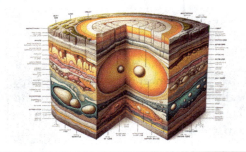
Instructional manual Instruction manuals often include detailed information about the product, including its specifications, features, components, and any technical details that may be relevant to the user.	

ILLUSTRATION STYLES	EXAMPLES
Botanical illustration A botanical illustration is a detailed and scientifically accurate artistic representation of a plant, flower, or botanical subject.	
Voynich manuscript It is named after Wilfrid Voynich, a Polish American bookseller who acquired the manuscript in 1912. The Voynich manuscript is famous for its unknown writing system and the numerous illustrations that have yet to be fully understood or explained.	
Mythological map A mythological map is a type of map that represents spaces, lands, or realms described in mythological narratives rather than real geographic locations.	
Scientific diagram Scientific diagrams serve the purpose of conveying complex information in a clear and concise visual format, making it easier for scientists, researchers, educators, and the general audience to understand scientific concepts and findings.	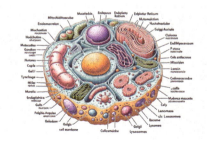

ILLUSTRATION STYLES	EXAMPLES
Voronoi diagram A Voronoi diagram, named after Russian mathematician Georgy Voronoi, is a way of dividing a space into a number of regions based on the distance to points in a specific subset of the space.	

Table 2.8: Illustration styles that are specifically instructional

Illustration styles that are specifically 3D and textured

When delving into 3D and textured illustration styles, we're exploring a realm where visuals are designed to exhibit depth, volume, and, often, a tangible feeling through the skillful use of shadows, highlights, and textures. Here are some examples:

ILLUSTRATION STYLES	EXAMPLES
Isometric 3D Isometric 3D, often referred to as isometric projection or isometric perspective, is a method of visually representing three-dimensional objects in two dimensions.	
Black velvet Black velvet is used in furniture upholstery to add a touch of luxury and sophistication to chairs, sofas, and cushions.	

ILLUSTRATION STYLES	EXAMPLES
3D render 3D rendering is a versatile and powerful tool that allows artists, designers, and professionals to bring their creative ideas to life, whether it's visualizing architectural designs, creating digital art, or producing stunning visual effects in movies and games.	
Scratch art Scratch art is a unique and creative art form that involves creating images by scratching away a top layer of material to reveal a contrasting color or surface beneath.	
Claymation Claymation is a form of animation in which characters and scenes are created by physically manipulating clay or plasticine figures and objects frame by frame to create the illusion of movement.	
Hama beads Hama beads, also known as Perler beads or fuse beads, are small, colorful plastic beads that are used in creative and craft projects.	

ILLUSTRATION STYLES	EXAMPLES
Felt pieces Felt pieces are often used for appliqué work, creating patches, embellishments, and decorations on clothing, accessories, and home textiles.	
Tattoo A tattoo is a permanent mark or design made on the skin by injecting ink or pigments into the dermal layer of the skin.	
Bronze statue Bronze statues are celebrated for their ability to capture the essence of a subject in a lasting and tangible form.	
Marble statue Sculptors often choose marble for its timeless beauty and the sense of permanence it imparts to their work.	

ILLUSTRATION STYLES	EXAMPLES
Sand sculpture A sand sculpture is a three-dimensional artwork created by shaping and carving sand into various shapes and designs.	
Plant sculpture These sculptures integrate living plants into artistic designs.	
Ice carving These sculptures are typically made from clear or colored ice and are admired for their intricate details, elegance, and the temporary nature of the medium.	

Table 2.9: Illustration styles that are specifically 3D and textured

Art movements

An art movement is a collective term that describes a specific trend or approach in art, often adopted by a group of artists who share common methodologies, philosophies, or aesthetic principles. These movements often reflect or respond to the cultural, social, and political dynamics of their time, providing unique lenses through which we can explore and interpret historical and societal shifts. A few notable art movements include the following:

ART MOVEMENTS	EXAMPLES
Surrealism Surrealism is a radical and influential movement that sought to explore and express the unconscious mind and the realm of dreams, defying rationality and conventional artistic norms.	
Pop art Pop art is an art movement that emerged in the 1950s, particularly in the United States and the United Kingdom. It is characterized by its bold and colorful depiction of everyday objects and popular culture.	
Cubism Objects are broken down into geometric shapes, such as cubes, spheres, cylinders, and cones.	
Neo-expressionism Neo-expressionism is an art movement that emerged in the late 1970s. It was a revival of painterly, expressive techniques in reaction to the conceptual and minimalist art that dominated the 1960s and 1970s.	

ART MOVEMENTS	EXAMPLES
Street art Street art is a form of visual art created in public locations, typically outside traditional art venues.	

Table 2.10: Art movements

Human elements

When we talk about "human elements," such as makeup, clothes, and hairstyles, in visual art and generation, we're referring to the incorporation of human-associated aesthetic and style attributes that can define, enhance, or even transform how a human figure is perceived in an image. Here are some examples:

HUMAN ELEMENTS	EXAMPLES
Costumes Costumes are designed to transform the wearer's appearance and help them embody a particular role or identity.	
Hairstyles Hairstyles play a significant role in appearance and can reflect individual preferences, cultural trends, and societal norms.	

HUMAN ELEMENTS	EXAMPLES
Shoes Sneakers are just one example of the different shoe styles you can create.	
Jewelry A diamond necklace is just one example of the jewelry you can create.	
Makeup Makeup is a transformative tool that allows individuals to express their creativity and experiment with different looks. You can experiment with different looks by adding more or less makeup.	

HUMAN ELEMENTS	EXAMPLES
Nail art Nail art is a popular way to add a touch of beauty and style to appearance. Here, you'll witness a mistake made by DALL-E 3! Hint: Look at the middle finger (generative art isn't perfect yet!).	

Table 2.11: Human elements

Places and settings

Places and settings in the context of image creation using DALL-E 3 refer to the physical and stylistic environments or locales that serve as the backdrop or focus of the generated images. These encompass various elements, each with its distinct attributes and characteristics. Here are some examples:

PLACES AND SETTINGS	EXAMPLES
Architecture Architecture is the art and science of designing and planning buildings and other physical structures.	
Stage sets Stage sets are an integral part of live theater, film, television, and other forms of visual storytelling.	

PLACES AND SETTINGS	EXAMPLES
Domestic interiors Domestic interiors encompass the design, layout, decoration, and furnishing of the interior spaces within a home.	
Cityscapes Cityscapes capture the essence and character of a city, showcasing its architectural landmarks, cultural diversity, and the interplay between human activity and the urban environment.	
Furniture Furniture is an integral part of interior design, and its selection and arrangement can greatly impact the functionality and aesthetics of a space.	

Table 2.12: Places and settings

While DALL-E 3 provides a robust platform for generating unique and creative images, further refinement and stylistic adjustments can be achieved using other specialized tools, such as Photoshop, Lightroom, or Instagram, for color correction and vintage effects. If you seek to infuse your DALL-E 3-generated image with a specific artistic style or detailed adjustments, utilizing these tools allows for a higher degree of control and precision. Through the use of DALL-E 3 and other image editing software, you can elevate your creation to closely match your envisioned aesthetic, ensuring a polished and artistically nuanced final piece.

Here are a few helpful words to get you experimenting with prompts that will enhance your outputs:

- **4K**: A 4K generative artwork has a high level of detail and clarity because of its increased pixel count. This can result in sharp and visually appealing images.

- **Macro 35mm film**: By adding the words "macro 35mm film" to the end of your prompt, your subject will now look like it's been shot with a 35mm macro lens.

- **3D Render**: A 3D render is a visual representation of a 3D object or environment that simulates how the object or scene would appear in the real world, taking into account factors such as lighting, materials, textures, and camera perspective. This is a great way to bring your ideas of interior design to life!

- **Action**: By adding the word "action" to your prompt, your subject will now be in an action position. Experiment by adding descriptive words to your prompt. For example, if your prompt is `photorealistic tabby cat`, you can add the word "`action`." Your prompt would be `photorealistic tabby cat, action..`

Now that we have gone through a huge variety of ways in which we can modify our prompts and, hence, our generated images, let's look at how we can save and share our creations.

Saving and sharing your image

Once you have crafted the images to your satisfaction, the subsequent step is to save your favored creations for future reference.

Figure 2.9: Saving and sharing your creation

Saving on the OpenAI platform

Saving your creation on the OpenAI platform is fairly easy:

1. Download the image by simply pressing the down arrow in the upper left corner (see *Figure 2.9*).

2. Name your file when you save it to your desktop or cloud.

The process of saving on Bing Image Creator is similar to the OpenAI platform. It only contains an additional step of adding your creation to a **collection**.

Saving on the Microsoft Bing Image Creator powered by DALL-E 3

These are the steps to save your creation on the Bing Image Creator:

1. Download by simply pressing the download button on the right side of the image (see *Figure 2.10*).

2. An additional step is to create a collection and save your image to the corresponding collection.

Figure 2.10: Saving images in Bing Creator

Sharing your creations from DALL-E 3 is designed to be both simple and accessible. By selecting the **Share** button, a link to your artwork is generated, which can be easily distributed through various channels such as email, text messages, or social media platforms. The process is straightforward, requiring just a copy and paste of the link to facilitate the sharing. Significantly, the recipient is not required to log in, ensuring they can view your creation hassle-free. Additionally, for offline viewing, downloading the image is a readily available option. This dual approach guarantees flexibility in how you choose to share your creative outputs with others.

Summary

In this chapter, you took steps toward mastering the initial creation process by learning how to articulate your ideas through precise text prompts. You got an insight into the iterative process of refining these images through revisions to match your envisioned concept perfectly.

You learned to save your crafted and refined images—the pivotal step to preserving and potentially sharing your creations. Along with individual image refinement, you also delved into the organizational feature of DALL-E 3 that enables you to save your works systematically into collections—enhancing the ease of access and categorization.

In the next chapter, we will look at creating variations and fine-tuning in DALL-E 3-generated images.

Summary

3

Variations and Fine-Tuning

In this chapter, we will delve into the specialized techniques of variations, parameters, and sizing within the context of AI-generated art. We will explore the creation and modification of images by generating multiple versions of an idea. The section on parameters and sizing will emphasize the importance of control over image attributes and quality.

We're going to cover the following main topics:

- Variations
- Parameters and sizing
- Inpainting and outpainting in DALL-E 2

By the end of this chapter, you will gain a deep and practical understanding of key processes in crafting AI art, which will allow you creative flexibility and empower you to explore, experiment, and fine-tune your creations with DALL-E.

Variations

Variations are slightly or significantly different versions of an image that can be created by altering that image's prompt. Creating variations of an image idea using DALL-E 3 is a powerful way to explore different perspectives of a single concept. Let's discuss how.

Variations in DALL-E 3 offer a rich landscape for exploration and refinement, letting creators iterate on initial concepts to arrive at a wide array of visually diverse outcomes. By tweaking the initial prompt, adjusting parameters, and using the tools available, users can navigate through countless permutations of their initial idea, breathing new life and perspectives into their creations with each variant. Now that we know what variations are, we will look at the systematic approach to creating variations in DALL-E 3.

Here's a step-by-step guide to creating variations in DALL-E 3:

1. **Access the DALL-E 3 interface**: Launch the DALL-E 3 interface and ensure you are logged in.

2. **Input initial prompt**: Begin by inputting a descriptive text prompt to represent your initial idea. Ensure the description is clear to guide DALL-E in generating an image that matches your vision.

3. **Generate initial image**: After inputting your prompt, initiate the image generation process. DALL-E will create an image based on the information contained in your prompt.

4. **Review the output**: Evaluate the initial output. If it doesn't fully satisfy your expectations, note the areas where changes are required.

5. **Modify the prompt**: To create variations, you can tweak the original prompt by changing or adding details, altering the style, perspective, or elements in the image description.

6. **Generate variations**: After making changes to the prompt, regenerate the image to see the new variation. Repeat this process multiple times, experimenting with different alterations to create a range of variations.

7. **Save your variations**: Once you have created a series of variations that you are happy with, save each variant individually to retain them for future reference.

8. **Create a collection**: Microsoft Bing Image Creator offers **Collections**, an area to organize your work, as we learned in *Chapter 2*. For better organization, create a collection where you can save all the variations together, providing a cohesive view of all the different perspectives derived from the original concept. Collections can only be saved if you are using the Bing Image Creator interface (OpenAI does not offer this feature). Bing only saves 20 sets of 4 images (80 images in total), before it overrides with your new images, so it is important to download and save any images that you want to keep.

9. **Share your creations**: After saving the variants in a collection, you can easily share the entire collection or individual variations with others through the **Share** option, which provides a link for sending via email, text, or social media. This feature is only available in Bing Image Creator (OpenAI does not offer this feature). If you are using OpenAI, you can download your image and send it via email or your preferred communication service/app.

10. **Feedback and adjustments**: If working in a collaborative environment, gather feedback from others and make further adjustments to perfect each variation based on the feedback received.

11. **Documentation**: Document the different stages of variations for a comprehensive view of your creative journey and to potentially aid in future projects.

Utilizing variations in DALL-E can serve several important functions, enhancing the image creation process both in terms of creativity and precision. Here are the primary reasons why using variations is beneficial:

- **Broadening your creative horizons**: By generating variations, users can explore a richer palette of potential outcomes. This allows for the discovery of unexpected and delightful results, some of which might be even better than originally envisioned.

- **Fine-tuning results**: Variations can facilitate a more meticulous crafting process. Users can generate a set of varied outcomes and then choose the one that aligns most closely with their vision, saving time and effort that might be spent on numerous individual generation attempts.

- **Enhancing detail and complexity**: Through variations, DALL-E can present a range of complexity and detail in the generated images. Users can select a result that has the right balance of detail and simplicity according to their preferences and the requirements of their project.

- **Avoiding monotonous outputs**: Relying on a single prompt might often yield monotonous or repetitive outputs. Variations introduce a dynamic element, presenting a range of styles and interpretations, thereby avoiding the trap of uniformity.

- **Expediting the iterative process**: The image creation process is often iterative. Variations provide a quick way to view multiple different iterations at once, helping users quickly home in on the best direction for their project.

- **Facilitating collaboration and feedback**: When working in a collaborative setting, having variations can be immensely helpful. It allows teams to review multiple options together, facilitating discussions and feedback and helping to reach a consensus on the best option to pursue.

- **Enhancing learning and experimentation**: For users who are in the learning phase, variations can offer a rich resource to understand DALL-E's capabilities and the impact of different prompts and settings, fostering a deeper understanding through experimentation.

In this examination of variations, we delved into a powerful feature of DALL-E 3 that facilitates the creation of a diverse range of outcomes from a single initial concept. This tool encourages users to iterate on their initial ideas, employing a series of tweaks of the original prompt and exploring different perspectives and styles, thereby enriching the original concept with new life and depth. This chapter serves as a gateway to mastering the art of creating variations, a journey of refined creativity. Next, we'll move on to parameters and sizing.

Parameters

DALL-E operates as a multimodal version of GPT-4, boasting a robust structure fortified with 12 billion parameters. This system *"exchanges text for pixels,"* leveraging a vast training dataset comprised of text-image pairs sourced from the internet to facilitate this interchange.

Multimodal

Multimodal in the context of DALL-E 3 refers to its ability to understand and generate content based on inputs from multiple types of data modes, particularly text and images. This is a significant aspect of its functionality and what makes it particularly powerful as an AI model.

Defining parameters in DALL-E is a pathway to creating highly personalized and unique images, lending your distinct touch to your creations. It's an exercise in artistic detail, where your vision guides the formulation of parameters that create visual narratives tuned to your creative preferences.

One of the best ways to get what you want when working with the parameters of DALL-E 3 is **prompt engineering**. This is the art of using generative AI to the fullest. Essentially, it involves a nuanced articulation of the desired outcome through text prompts, effectively directing DALL-E to conjure images that align with your vision.

Prompt engineering stands, potentially, as the most pivotal aspect when it comes to molding the exact AI image you envision. The potency of prompt engineering lies in its depth and flexibility, allowing users to explore a rich tapestry of possibilities through textual descriptions that are both elaborate and precise.

The secret to getting great results with AI is finding the right mix of being clear but also letting the AI be creative. If you're not specific enough, the AI might create something totally different from what you wanted. But if you're too detailed, you might limit how creative the AI can be. So, to get the best out of AI, you need to know how to explain your ideas clearly but also give the AI some space to add its own creative touch.

Prompt engineering fosters a space for iterative enhancements; users can constantly refine their prompts based on the AI's responses, moving closer to the perfect depiction with each iteration. This iterative process essentially forms a feedback loop, allowing the user to understand the AI's interpretation pathway and steer it in the desired direction.

> **Feedback loop**
> A feedback loop is a process where the outcomes of a system are reused as inputs, allowing the system to modify its actions based on past performance, leading to continuous improvement or maintaining a certain state.

Iterations enable users to explore different styles, moods, and settings. This meticulous crafting and refinement of prompts become a canvas for users, offering a realm where they can paint with words to create images that are rich, detailed, and aligned with their artistic vision.

In essence, prompt engineering stands as a testimony to the limitless potential that can be unlocked when one learns to harness the full power of articulation in guiding AI imagery generation. If you learn one thing about generative AI, it should be how to use prompt engineering well!

Let's understand prompt engineering better with an example.

In this example, we will consider the prompt "dog's nose" and test it against the prompt "close-up of dog's nose, golden hour, 35mm film."

In *Figure 3.1*, adding the words "golden hour" to the prompt evoked the look of the sun going down by adding the warm golden light that I wanted in the image.

In this scenario, both look like they were photographed with 35mm film, but that's not always the case when an image is generated. When you don't specify certain details such as "35mm film" in your prompt, the AI has more creative freedom and might produce a variety of styles, including painted or surreal looks. In this case, it just happened to come out looking like a photo even with the original prompt.

Figure 3.1: Adding the words "golden hour" to the prompt "dog's nose" results appear in "35mm film" style

The following is another example of how prompt engineering can make a difference to the output. In this case, we use the prompt "pinto horse on a beach."

You'll see the difference when you add specific terms, such as the style of the shot and lighting, to the prompt. Here, we added movement and lighting by using the terms "running" and "golden hour," producing this prompt: "pinto horse running on a beach, golden hour."

Figure 3.2: Adding the words "running" and "golden hour" to the prompt "pinto horse on a beach"

Now that you understand how to use parameters to iterate and create an enhanced image, let's now turn our attention to the aspect of sizing.

Sizing

In DALL-E 3, all generated images inherently have a square format with their dimensions set to **1024 x 1024 pixels (px)**. However, if you include the size in your prompt, you can create an image of the sizes **1792px by 1024px** or **1024px by 1792px**.

Let's consider an example.

In *Figure 3.3*, we use the prompt:

```
Create a coffee mug that says, "TODAY is the BEST day!" make it
1792px by 1024px.
```

Figure 3.3: Image from the prompt, Create a coffee mug that says,
"TODAY is the BEST day!" make it 1792px by 1024px

Alternatively, if the sizing isn't specified, the default will be **1024px x 1024px**, as you'll notice in the following figure.

Figure 3.4: Another iteration of the prompt in Figure 3.3

The image size used by DALL-E 3 (at the time of publishing of this book) can be used to create prints up to **20" x 11.5"** or **12" x 12"** while maintaining a crisp image. See *Figure 3.5*, which shows an image of a sloth that I designed and uploaded to my Fine Art America account. This image can be utilized for art prints, coffee mugs, and various other merchandise. We will discuss more about printing your images on merchandise in detail in the next chapter.

Figure 3.5: Print size for merchandise on Fine Art America

Now that you know how to adjust sizing within your prompts, let's turn our attention to inpainting and outpainting, which were available for a short time on the OpenAI platform, and I hope they bring them back!

Inpainting and outpainting in DALL-E 2

Open AI offered inpainting and outpainting as additional features for a short time on DALL-E 2. Inpainting and outpainting are two distinct processes in image processing and computer graphics that deal with the restoration or generation of image content.

Inpainting is the process of filling in missing or corrupted parts of an image with plausible data derived from the surrounding pixels. Using the inpainting feature in DALL-E 2 allowed users to repair damaged areas of an image or fill in missing parts with content generated based on the surrounding area.

Outpainting is the process of extending the boundaries of an image by generating new content around the existing canvas based on the contextual information of the current image content. This feature allowed users to extend the boundaries of an existing image, generating additional content seamlessly connected to the outer edges of the original canvas.

These features were an enormously powerful tool in the creative process using DALL-E 2. Unfortunately, inpainting and outpainting are not accessible in DALL-E 3 at the time of writing. We hope that OpenAI brings these features back.

Summary

In this chapter, we learned about the critical components that facilitate the optimal use of DALL-E 3: parameters, prompt engineering, and sizing. We discovered parameters and prompt engineering—sophisticated skills—where textual inputs guide the AI to hone the generation process, bringing a conceptual vision into reality. Lastly, we learned how to control image sizing. Together, these three elements form a triad that empowers users to navigate DALL-E 3 effectively.

In the next chapter, we will discuss how to create fine art prints with DALL-E 3.

Part 2: Practical Applications

In the next sections, you'll learn how to use DALL-E to craft fine art prints, explore the integration of AI art with **Non-Fungible Tokens (NFTs)** for digital marketing, and discover the art of designing engaging covers for various publications. These chapters are tailored to equip you with the knowledge to bring digital art into the physical world, navigate the digital marketplace, and create striking visuals that tell a story.

This part has the following chapters:

- *Chapter 4, Crafting Fine Art Prints with DALL-E 3*
- *Chapter 5, DALL-E 3 and the World of NFTs*
- *Chapter 6, Designing Art for Covers of Books, Magazines, and Other Publications*

4

Crafting Fine Art Prints with DALL-E 3

In this chapter, we step into the fascinating realm of artistry where the digital meets the physical, as we navigate through the intricate process of transforming your DALL-E 3 creations into tangible fine art prints. We will meticulously explore the bridging of two worlds: the innovative generation of images with DALL-E 3, and the classic allure of physical art pieces, giving form and frame to your digital creations through a reputable fulfillment center such as Fine Art America, or your choice of a fulfillment center.

We'll commence our journey by discussing the pivotal steps of refining and preparing DALL-E 3-generated images for print. Ensuring that the ethereal quality and intricate details of your digital art are not lost in translation from pixels to print is paramount, and thus, we'll cover the essential techniques for image optimization and format selection.

Next, we'll delve into the realm of Fine Art America, a platform that will metamorphose your digital wonders into physical art forms, be framed print, canvas, or other mediums. From the nuances of choosing the right print material to aligning your aesthetic vision with practical production, every step will be illuminated with a practical guide.

We'll be covering these concepts under the following main topics:

- Creating with print in mind
- Uploading to a print-on-demand platform
- Sharing your art

Technical requirements

Navigate to your selected online fulfillment center when your art is primed for upload. In this chapter, we'll utilize Fine Art America for demonstration purposes. Proceed to the designated URL once your creation is prepped and polished for the next step in its journey from digital to tangible: `https://fineartamerica.com/`.

Creating with print in mind

The mindset of creating art with print in mind is indispensable for digital artists, tech enthusiasts, and traditional creatives alike. Art created with print in mind bridges the divide between the world of **artificial intelligence** (**AI**) and the tactile world we inhabit.

Let's begin this journey to a new horizon in artistic expression, where your creations can be touched, held, and felt, transforming spaces and perceptions in the most intimate way possible.

To create print-ready art, we will want to consider the three Cs: **concept**, **composition**, and **coloration**. Let's look at these three Cs to success.

Exploring the three Cs to success

To create art that is both true to our vision and commercially viable, we use the three Cs framework. Understanding how to apply the formula of concept, composition, and coloration helps in blending our inspiration with a market-friendly formula, ensuring both artistic integrity and sales success.

Concept

Determining the best digital art concept to create for sales involves a mix of understanding market trends, recognizing your unique artistic strengths, and considering your target audience. Here are some steps to help guide your decision:

- **Research current trends**: Look at platforms such as Google Trends, ArtStation, DeviantArt, and social media to see what types of digital art are currently popular. This can include specific themes, styles, or subjects. For example, you can go to Google Trends right now and gain insights into what the current shopping trends are in real time. What's trending now can serve as inspiration for your own artwork.

- **Identify your strengths**: Reflect on your own skills and style. What type of digital art do you excel at? Is there a unique style or subject matter you are particularly good at?

- **Understand your audience**: Who is your target market? Different audiences may prefer different types of art. For example, younger audiences might be more drawn to vibrant, contemporary styles, while other groups might prefer more traditional or abstract art.

- **Analyze market demand**: Use platforms such as Etsy, Society6, or Redbubble to see what is selling well. Look for patterns in the types of artwork that are popular and well received.

- **Consider the purpose**: Are you creating art for decorative purposes, such as prints and posters, or for more commercial uses, such as game art or book covers? The intended use can greatly influence the type of art you create.

- **Experiment and innovate**: Don't be afraid to try something new or mix different styles. Sometimes, the most successful art pieces are those that break the mold.

- **Get feedback**: Share your ideas or preliminary sketches with peers, potential customers, or on social media to gauge interest and get feedback.

- **Stay true to your vision**: While it's important to understand the market, it's equally important to create art that resonates with you. Authenticity often shines through and can be a key selling point.

- **Monitor your success**: Once you start selling, keep track of which pieces do well and try to understand why. This can help inform your future creations.

- **Keep learning**: The digital art world is always evolving. Stay up to date with new software, ideas, and techniques.

Composition

The composition of digital art plays a crucial role in its appeal and marketability, balancing the dichotomy between traditional artistic fundamentals and the cutting-edge capabilities of modern technology.

While bridging this gap, it is essential to consider how these artworks appeal to the human eye and mind, crafting experiences that resonate on both a visual and cerebral level.

Appeal to the human eye and mind

To truly grasp what kind of art captivates the human eye and mind, it's important to look into key aspects that forge a deep connection with the viewer. These include the following:

- **Visual harmony**: Good composition creates a visually pleasing balance by using elements such as color, line, form, and texture. This harmony is essential in catching and retaining the viewer's attention.

- **Storytelling**: Composition can convey narratives or emotions, creating a deeper connection with the viewer. This can be particularly powerful in digital art, where technology allows for more dynamic and immersive storytelling.

- **Psychological impact**: Certain compositional techniques, such as the use of leading lines or the **rule of thirds**, can guide the viewer's eye in a specific way, creating a psychological impact and enhancing the overall experience.

> **Note**
>
> The rule of thirds is a fundamental principle in the field of visual arts, used to create balanced and visually appealing compositions. This rule involves dividing an image into nine equal parts by drawing two equally spaced horizontal lines and two equally spaced vertical lines across the image. This grid effectively splits the canvas or frame into thirds, both horizontally and vertically. According to the rule of thirds, the most important elements or focal points of the composition should be placed along these lines or at their intersections. These points are known as the points of interest. The idea behind this is that an off-center composition is more pleasing to the eye and appears more natural than one where the subject is placed directly in the middle.

Target audience appeal

In the realm of artistic creation, understanding your audience is paramount. By aligning your art with the preferences and cultural nuances of your intended market, you significantly enhance its relevance and appeal. Here we will explore two critical aspects to consider:

- **Demographic preferences**: Different audiences may have varying preferences in terms of style, color schemes, and subjects. Understanding these preferences is key to creating compositions that resonate with the intended market. With just a little investigation, you can have a large impact on the acceptance of your art.

- **Cultural resonance**: Composition can include cultural elements that appeal to specific groups, making the artwork more relatable and appealing to those audiences.

Traditional basics versus latest-generation technology

In the dynamic landscape of art, the interplay between time-honored principles and cutting-edge technology plays a crucial role. This section looks into how the foundational elements of traditional art merged with the innovative capabilities of modern technology, creating a new realm of possibilities for artists. Let's explore this synergy through the following aspects:

- **Traditional art principles**: The basics of good composition in traditional art—balance, contrast, focus, movement, proportion, rhythm, and unity—are still relevant in digital art. These principles form the foundation upon which digital artistry is built. When in doubt, go back to the basics for inspiration and clarity.

- **Technology-enhanced possibilities**: Modern technology offers tools that expand the possibilities of composition. For example, 3D modeling, virtual reality, and algorithm-based art can create compositions that were unimaginable in traditional mediums. You can use any form of technology to inspire you in your digital art. Don't limit yourself!

- **Blending old and new**: Successful digital artists often blend traditional compositional techniques with modern technological advancements. This creates art that is both rooted in foundational artistic wisdom and expressive of contemporary possibilities.

Marketing and selling digital art

Navigating the digital art market requires not just creativity but also a keen understanding of how to effectively present and adapt your work in the digital realm. This section focuses on strategies for making your digital art more appealing and marketable in an increasingly online world. Consider the following key points:

- **Visual impact in digital spaces**: In a digital marketplace, the initial visual impact of a composition is key to capturing interest. Compelling compositions stand out in digital galleries or online platforms.

- **Adaptability across platforms**: A good digital composition translates well across various digital platforms, from online galleries to social media, enhancing its marketability.

The composition of digital art is a delicate balance between adhering to time-honored artistic principles and embracing the boundless possibilities offered by modern technology. It's this blend that captivates both the human eye and the digital market, making composition a central factor in the success and salability of digital art.

Colorization

Colorization plays a crucial role in designing digital art, especially when the objective is to sell the artwork. Here are several key aspects of how color choice can significantly enhance or degrade a digital art piece:

- **Emotional impact**: Colors have a profound effect on human emotions and perceptions. For instance, warm colors such as red and orange can evoke feelings of warmth, passion, or energy, while cool colors such as blue and green tend to be calming and soothing. Selecting the right color palette can help convey the desired emotional tone of the artwork and connect with the audience on an emotional level that you are trying to achieve.

- **Visual appeal and aesthetics**: The choice of colors can make an artwork visually appealing or off-putting. Understanding **color theory** is vital to the success of any piece of art. Harmonious color combinations are pleasing to the eye and can draw viewers in while clashing or overly bright colors can be jarring and repulsive. The use of complementary colors, analogous colors, or monochromatic schemes can greatly enhance the aesthetic appeal of the piece. The choice of color palette is a primary decision one must make before getting deep into the creative process.

- **Theme and atmosphere**: Colors can set the tone and atmosphere of a piece. Darker colors might be used to create a moody, mysterious feel, while brighter, vibrant colors can create a sense of excitement and energy. The right color choices help in establishing the theme and setting the mood of the artwork.

- **Focus and composition**: Strategic use of color can guide the viewer's eye to the focal points of the artwork. High contrast areas and unique color choices can draw attention to key elements, enhancing the overall composition and storytelling aspect of the piece.

- **Cultural and contextual relevance**: Colors have different meanings and associations in various cultures. For instance, white is associated with purity in some cultures, but with mourning in others. Being mindful of these associations is crucial, especially when targeting a diverse or international market. As we discussed in the previous section, understanding your target audience is crucial.

- **Branding and marketability**: In the context of commercial art, color choices should align with the branding and marketing goals. Colors that resonate with the target audience and align with the brand identity can make the art more appealing to potential buyers.

- **Trends and popularity**: Staying aware of color trends in the art and design world can also influence the salability of digital art. Trendy colors can make the artwork more appealing to contemporary buyers. Conversely, using a different pallet can, if thoughtfully applied, help your art stand out from the norm.

- **Psychological effects**: Some colors have been found to have psychological effects; for example, blue is often seen as trustworthy, which might be beneficial for certain themes. Having a solid understanding of color theory is extraordinarily helpful in achieving your desired result, connection, or emotion. You can learn the basics of color theory here: `https://packt.link/seqJx`.

- **Quality and professionalism**: Skillful use of color can demonstrate the artist's expertise and the quality of the work. Poor color choices, on the other hand, can make the artwork look amateurish, affecting its market value. Experiment with DALL-E 3 and see what different colors emote with a similar picture. Once you determine what color theme you want to use, you can use it in your prompt.

Colorization is not just about making art visually pleasing; it's about effectively communicating emotions, themes, and messages, enhancing the storytelling aspect of the art, and aligning with your strategies to appeal to the target audience. The right color choices can significantly elevate the value and appeal of digital art, making it more likely to sell.

As we've discussed, the quality and marketability of digital art heavily depend on its concept, composition, and colorization. A unique and engaging concept attracts the audience's interest, setting the artwork's theme and direction, and composition is crucial for guiding the viewer's eye and enhancing visual appeal.

Having explored how colorization significantly influences the design and appeal of digital art, we now turn our attention to another burgeoning domain in the digital art world: creating AI art for resale.

Finding your niche and creating AI art for resale

Establishing a distinctive artistic style is paramount when endeavoring to sell your artwork, particularly in a market replete with diverse talents and creations. Your style isn't just a representation of your skills; it's an intimate glance into your artistic soul, the themes that drive your passion, and the unique lens through which you perceive the world. Here's why this signature touch is so crucial:

- **Recognition and branding**: Much like a brand, your style sets you apart, making your artwork immediately recognizable. This recognition can create a sense of consistency and trust among your audience, similar to a visual signature that becomes synonymous with your name and quality of work.

- **Emotional connection**: Art is profoundly personal, and buyers often seek pieces that resonate with them on an emotional level. A consistent artistic style speaks in a language that your audience understands and feels connected to, often leading to a deeper, more personal engagement with your work.

- **Professionalism and seriousness**: Artists with a defined style often project a higher degree of professionalism and dedication to their craft. It reflects the time and effort taken to hone their skills and understand their artistic desires, which can be very appealing to art collectors.

- **Narrative and depth**: Your style is the story you tell, woven through all your pieces. Collectors aren't just buying a piece of art; they're buying a chapter of your artistic journey. A certain style gives depth to this story, inviting your audience to be part of a larger narrative.

- **Niche creation**: A unique style helps you carve out your niche in a crowded marketplace. This niche attracts a specific audience, making your art more desirable to those who feel a connection to the work you create.

However, it's important to balance consistency with evolution. An artistic style shouldn't be a limitation, but rather a solid foundation upon which you can explore and expand your creative expressions.

While a certain style helps establish your artistic identity, continuous growth and adaptation ensure that your art remains dynamic, relevant, and true to your journey. Pay attention to the subjects that ignite your passion or provoke deep thought and emotion in you. Concurrently, assess the art market. Identify gaps or specific areas that pique your interest, and explore how your unique approach can fill these spaces in a way no one else has approached.

Don't shy away from experimentation; it's through trial and error that you'll discover what feels authentic to you and what resonates with others. Engage with your audience, other artists, and critics to receive feedback, but also, stay true to your artistic voice. Analyze what artworks have been well received and why, but don't lose your essence chasing trends.

Remember, a niche isn't just where your art fits; it's where your creativity thrives, pushing boundaries and challenging norms.

The artistic spectrum of DALL-E 3

DALL-E 3, is specifically designed to generate images from textual descriptions, showcasing an impressive ability to conceptualize and produce images that match specific, often complex, textual inputs. However, its capabilities have certain limitations and nuances in terms of the range of artistic styles it can reproduce or create. Here are some examples of AI terms you might hear in the art world:

- **Generative art**: DALL-E 3 can generate art from descriptions—aligning with generative art principles. Generative art is a type of art where the artist creates a set of rules or uses a tool such as a computer program or machine. This system then operates on its own to some extent, helping to create the final artwork. The principles of generative art are often based on the foundational elements of the system being used, such as algorithms or rules applied to produce new artworks.

- **Neural paintings**: DALL-E 3 excels at creating images—including detailed, painterly ones— from textual descriptions, which could be considered akin to neural paintings. Neural paintings refer to artworks created with the help of neural networks, a type of AI. These neural networks are algorithms modeled on the human brain, designed to recognize patterns and generate new content based on the data they've been trained on. In the context of art, neural networks can analyze styles, techniques, and elements from existing artworks and then use this knowledge to create new, unique paintings. This process often involves an element of randomness and machine learning, resulting in innovative and sometimes unexpected artistic outputs. Neural paintings are part of the broader field of AI-generated art, where technology and creativity intersect. While both generative art and neural painting involve the use of technology to create art, generative art is broader and focuses more on the autonomous system and process that creates the art, often involving a degree of randomness. In contrast, neural painting is specifically about using AI and neural networks to create or modify images, often focusing on the AI's learned ability to mimic or innovate upon existing artistic styles. Here is an example: imagine an artist has a vision of a painting that combines the swirling starry night sky reminiscent of Van Gogh's *Starry Night* with a serene landscape featuring a calm river and a cherry blossom tree, a scene that doesn't exist in any photograph or painting they have access to.

- **AI-assisted art**: Artists might use DALL-E 3 to generate ideas, concepts, or elements that they can incorporate into their work. AI-assisted art refers broadly to any art project where AI plays a role in the creation process, often serving as a tool or assistant to the human artist. The AI can help in various tasks, such as suggesting composition, enhancing or adjusting colors, or even helping to render realistic details, but it's generally under the direct guidance of the artist.

In essence, while all three involve a synergy between technology and art, AI-assisted art is more about AI helping humans create, generative art is about systems creating art based on predefined rules or algorithms, and neural painting is centered around AI systems creating visual art, often with some level of human guidance or collaboration.

In *Chapter 2*, we discussed how DALL-E 3 can be prompted with various mediums such as pencil sketches, charcoal, watercolor, line art, and more. Remember, these can become signature elements of your style. You might decide to exclusively use watercolor prompts or lean into impressionistic styles. You could also stick with a certain angle (e.g., low angle), lighting style (such as low-key lighting), or a particular film type (such as Kodachrome), carving out your unique artistic voice.

My personal preference is to use a photorealistic style and mainly use dogs or cats as subjects in my artwork. You might establish a unique style and consistent subject matter across your creations, ensuring that your artistic signature is recognizable. When people see your pieces, they'll immediately know they're yours, thanks to the distinctive style and themes you consistently showcase.

Uploading to a print-on-demand platform

Print-on-demand stores are one of the fastest ways to monetize your AI art. As mentioned earlier in the chapter, we will be using Fine Art America as the print-on-demand platform in this chapter. You can create an account on Fine Art America or any other fulfillment center of your choice. I prefer Fine Art America because it's easy to use for both the artist and the buyer. You also have the option of being paid via PayPal. Thousands of independent artists worldwide use this platform to create millions of unique products, such as art prints on paper, canvas, shirts, and coffee mugs. To get started, you'll fill out the appropriate registration form and in less than one minute, you'll be up and running with a free account.

After setting up your account, you can begin uploading your art, very simply, by following these steps:

1. Click the **Upload Image** button, as seen in *Figure 4.1*.

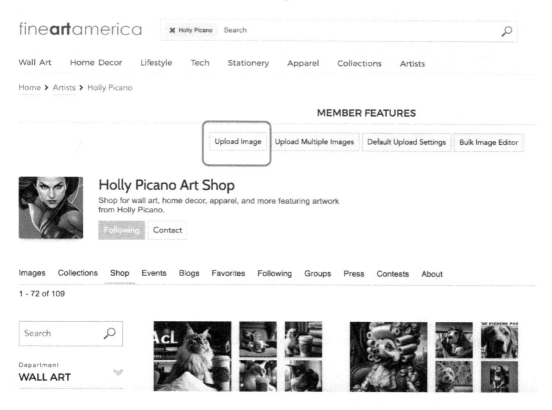

Figure 4.1: Fine Art America upload

2. Choose the **Choose File** option, then select your image, and click **Upload Image** again.
3. Complete the image details, such as title, description, and price, then click **SUBMIT**, as seen in *Figure 4.2*.

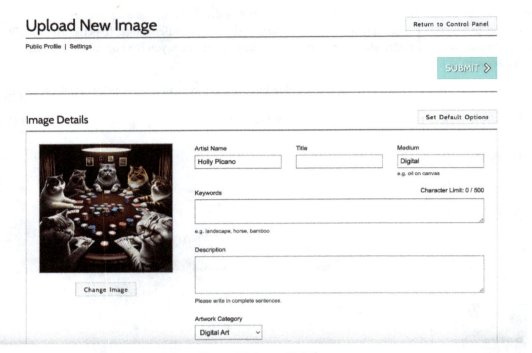

Figure 4.2: Image Details

Here's the fantastic news: the moment you upload your artwork to Fine Art America, it becomes immediately available for purchase! That's right, instant exposure to a global marketplace the second your art graces the platform.

Imagine the feeling of excitement knowing that right after you click **SUBMIT**, your art can be discovered, appreciated, and even end up as someone's prized possession. No waiting periods and no approval delays; your art is instantly out there in front of millions of potential buyers from all corners of the globe.

This immediate availability is not just about selling; it's about opportunities. It's about your artwork crossing borders and breaking boundaries. And, of course, it's about building your career, your brand, and your future in the art world.

One of the unique aspects of Fine Art America is its intuitive system that automatically determines the printable size of your images. That's right, no guesswork or complicated calculations on your part! Once you upload your artwork, the platform immediately analyzes its resolution and lets you know the maximum size it can be effectively printed. This ensures that your art maintains its clarity and integrity, guaranteeing a high-quality print every time. Take a look at the following example in *Figure 4.3*, which shows that an artwork is available in three different sizes.

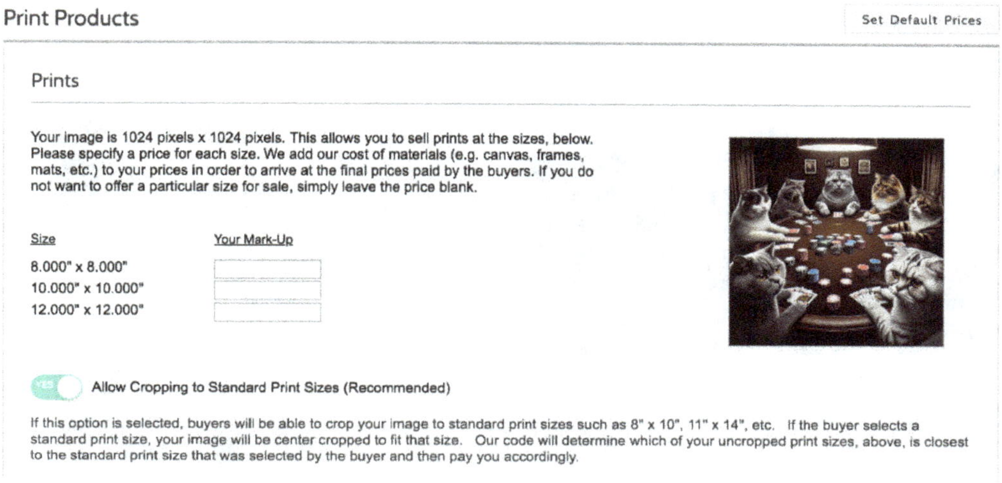

Print Products   Set Default Prices

Prints

Your image is 1024 pixels x 1024 pixels. This allows you to sell prints at the sizes, below. Please specify a price for each size. We add our cost of materials (e.g. canvas, frames, mats, etc.) to your prices in order to arrive at the final prices paid by the buyers. If you do not want to offer a particular size for sale, simply leave the price blank.

Size   Your Mark-Up
8.000" x 8.000"
10.000" x 10.000"
12.000" x 12.000"

[YES] Allow Cropping to Standard Print Sizes (Recommended)

If this option is selected, buyers will be able to crop your image to standard print sizes such as 8" x 10", 11" x 14", etc. If the buyer selects a standard print size, your image will be center cropped to fit that size. Our code will determine which of your uncropped print sizes, above, is closest to the standard print size that was selected by the buyer and then pay you accordingly.

Figure 4.3: Fine Art America prints

Your art is not just confined to traditional formats such as paper or canvas (though those options are available and popular!). Fine Art America opens the door to a world of possibilities, allowing your designs to be printed on a plethora of merchandise. Imagine your artwork coming to life on everyday items such as tote bags, bringing beauty to someone's daily shopping trip, or coffee mugs, adding a touch of art to those quiet moments people spend with their favorite beverage. It's about integrating your visions into daily life, making art accessible, and your creations forming a connection with people in their everyday routines.

Apart from being a comprehensive online marketplace and providing a fulfillment service, it is dedicated to empowering artists through innovative sales and marketing tools designed to simplify and propel their careers forward.

One of the standout features is the ability for artists to establish their own branded web stores; see *Figure 4.4*. This means you can create a professional-looking, easily accessible hub for your art that reflects your personal brand, all while leveraging the extensive audience that Fine Art America attracts. Artists can directly engage with the burgeoning market on social media platforms, such as selling their art prints through Facebook and Instagram, truly meeting potential buyers where they are. Additionally, this platform helps artists connect with their audience through tools such as e-newsletter creation, allowing them to maintain valuable relationships with their collectors, and inform them about new works, exhibitions, or any upcoming events.

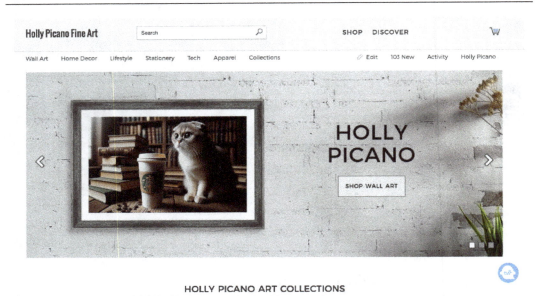

Figure 4.4: Fine Art America artist page

What's truly inspiring is that you're joining a community of over 100,000 living artists who collectively offer 10 million images for sale on `fineartamerica.com`. This isn't just a marketplace; it's a thriving ecosystem of creative individuals dedicated to their craft, sharing their worldview through art, and enriching lives by making art accessible and commonplace.

Now that you have learned how to create your art and upload it to a fulfillment center, in the next section, we will talk more about sharing the art that you created and uploaded.

Using Fine Art America

Fine Art America emerges as a versatile platform, amalgamating the functions of multiple services into a single, efficient entity. In the previous heading, we discussed its role as an art marketplace, but it is more than that. It's a resourceful environment where artists are afforded the tools to build and control their digital portfolios effectively.

Creating your portfolio

This platform facilitates artists in creating their own specialized websites, a digital space where their portfolio can breathe and grow, unconfined from the norms of traditional galleries. It's a space that's uniquely theirs, allowing for direct engagement with enthusiasts and collectors. Also, with the integration of email marketing tools, artists can foster and maintain deeper connections with their audience, keeping them abreast of new creations, shows, or any upcoming events.

The sphere of influence for an artist is no longer limited to galleries and exhibitions thanks to integrated social media functionalities. These ensure that artworks can transcend traditional boundaries and reach audiences globally, inviting a wider, more diverse dialogue around their work.

Finding the features

Accessing your features is straightforward and centralized, primarily located on the **Settings** page. To navigate there, locate your name positioned in the upper-right corner of the interface, as shown in *Figure 4.5*. Upon clicking your name, a drop-down menu will appear; select **Settings** from this list. This action will direct you to a comprehensive page brimming with various options available for your utilization.

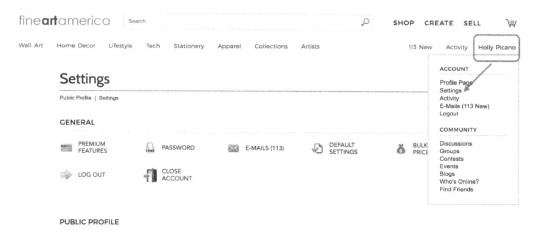

Figure 4.5: Finding your settings

In this resource-rich section, you'll be able to write your biography, set up your email lists, set your bulk prices, and upload your profile picture. Speaking of profile pictures, if you're reading this book, I'm certain you'll want to try an AI portrait of yourself, because why not? If you want to keep up with your analytics and statistics, you can see how many visitors you've had, how many of them commented on your artwork, and how many have favorited your artwork. The analytics are a great way to see what's hot and what's not!

Using augmented reality

The platform also offers features such as **augmented reality (AR)** apps. These apps allow individuals to visualize pieces within their own spaces before making a purchase, thereby personalizing and enhancing the buyer's journey. Go to *Figure 4.6* to see how AR technology works, as we place a painting on the wall using AR. It's a "try before you buy" feature.

Figure 4.6: Using AR to "try before you buy"

In essence, the platform represents a new era where technology and art coalesce, providing a multifunctional platform that supports artists in various aspects, from showcasing their work and widening their reach to directly engaging with their audience. It's a contemporary solution for the modern artist, adapting to the ever-evolving digital landscape of the art world.

Sharing on social media

Once you upload an image, you'll see options to share on Instagram, Facebook, X (formerly Twitter), and Pinterest on the right-hand side of your image. See *Figure 4.7* for sharing options. There is also code that you can copy and embed on your website or anywhere else you can use code. This option is also on the right-hand side of your image.

Figure 4.7: Sharing your image

Underneath the social sharing buttons, you will be able to see the different options viewers have to purchase your items. They select what they want (a canvas, a print, a framed print, a bag, or a mug) and have it shipped directly to their home. There's no need for you to do anything else; the fulfillment center does it for you!

Guides and tutorials

In the **About Us** section, you'll discover guides and tutorials essential for navigating the online marketplace, establishing your unique footprint, and optimizing your presence. It includes insightful information on integrating shopping cart widgets, allowing you to feature and sell your art seamlessly across various websites. Additionally, if you're utilizing platforms such as Shopify or WordPress, you'll find valuable guidance on e-commerce drop fulfillment. There's also a wealth of knowledge on strategizing and executing email campaigns, as well as orchestrating limited-time promotions to boost your visibility and sales.

Summary

In this chapter, we delved into the art of creating with print production in mind, focusing on several critical aspects. Firstly, we embraced the three Cs: concept, composition, and color, ensuring our creations are visually compelling and coherent. We also paid close attention to potential buyers' preferences, aiming to strike a balance between popular trends and individual tastes.

Additionally, we covered the practical steps of digital art entrepreneurship. This includes setting up a profile with an online fulfillment center, a crucial move for managing production and distribution efficiently. We learned how to upload our artwork to these platforms, making sure it's presented in the best possible light.

We discussed the importance of marketing our artwork. Using various channels such as email marketing and social media platforms, we learned strategies to effectively share our art with a wider audience, thereby increasing visibility and potential sales.

In the next chapter, we'll transition to a cutting-edge topic in the digital art world: creating AI art for use as **non-fungible tokens** (**NFTs**). We'll discuss how AI-generated art can be minted as NFTs, exploring the nuances of this digital frontier, and how it intersects with concepts such as blockchain, digital ownership, and the evolving landscape of art in the digital age.

5

DALL-E 3 and the World of NFTs

In this chapter, we will learn about the intersection of DALL-E 3 and **non-fungible tokens** (**NFTs**). We will understand how to mint AI-generated artwork as NFTs, exploring the basics of blockchain technology, the minting process, and platforms for NFT transactions. This knowledge will empower you to enter the world of NFT art, potentially unlocking new ways to monetize their AI-generated creations. By the end of this chapter, you'll be able to do the following:

- Create AI art for NFTs

- Create collections

- Upload to an NFT platform

> **Disclaimer**
> Creating an NFT can be a rewarding experience, but it's important to be aware of the costs and risks involved, as well as the fluctuating nature of the cryptocurrency and NFT markets.

Technical requirements

In this section, we will use DALL-E 3 on Microsoft Bing Image Creator because it offers an easier way to keep your work organized within collections. Organizing your work in this way will make it easier and more efficient to determine which of your designs you will keep for your NFT project. Get started here:

- Use Bing Image Creator (`https://www.bing.com/images/create`) to create images and organize them into collections of work

- You will also need to use an NFT platform such as the following:

  - **OpenSea**: `https://opensea.io/`

  - **Rarible**: `https://rarible.com/`

  - **Binance**: `https://www.binance.com/en-IN/nft/home`

For this chapter, we will be using OpenSea, which launched in 2017 and hosts many popular NFTs. This platform is a solid choice as it offers an uncomplicated marketplace.

Understanding NFTs

An NFT is a unique digital asset that represents ownership or proof of authenticity of a unique item or piece of content, primarily using blockchain technology.

> **Blockchain technology**
>
> Blockchain technology is a secure, decentralized system that records transactions across many computers, ensuring data integrity. It consists of interconnected blocks containing transaction data, secured through cryptographic hashes. This technology enables transparent and direct transactions without intermediaries, supporting uses beyond cryptocurrencies, such as **supply chain management (SCM)** and digital identity verification, by offering an efficient framework for data verification and exchange.

Unlike cryptocurrencies such as *Bitcoin* or *Ethereum*, which are fungible and can be exchanged on a one-to-one basis, each NFT is distinct and cannot be exchanged on a like-for-like basis, hence the term "non-fungible."

Some notable NFTs include Beeple's *Everydays: the First 5000 Days* and the *Bored Ape Yacht Club (BAYC)*. Each has garnered popularity for specific reasons and achieved remarkable sale prices.

Beeple's **Everydays: the First 5000 Days**, a digital collage representing 5,000 days of consecutive artwork, made headlines for its record-breaking sale at 69.3 million USD. Its popularity stems not only from the staggering sale price but also from Beeple's reputation and the piece's embodiment of the digital art evolution over more than a decade.

BAYC, a collection of 10,000 unique Ethereum-based NFTs, each depicting apes with various traits and accessories, has become a symbol of status and community in the NFT space. The exclusivity of owning a BAYC NFT, which grants access to a private community and real-world events, coupled with celebrity endorsements, has significantly driven its popularity. While individual BAYC NFTs have sold for varying amounts, some have fetched millions of dollars, reflecting their high demand and the project's overall prestige in the NFT market.

Key characteristics of NFTs include the following:

- **Uniqueness**: Each NFT has distinct properties. This uniqueness is often verified through digital signatures. A **digital signature** is a cryptographic technique that verifies the authenticity and integrity of a digital document or message, ensuring it has not been tampered with and confirming the identity of the sender.

- **Digital ownership**: NFTs confer digital ownership or rights to the holder. This can be ownership of a digital artwork, collectible, or other forms of digital content.

- **Indivisibility**: NFTs typically cannot be divided into smaller units. You buy, sell, and own the entire NFT.

- **Interoperability**: NFTs can be traded or moved across various ecosystems due to the standardized token protocol on which they are built, predominantly Ethereum.

- **Immutability and provenance**: Once an NFT is created, its data, including ownership and transaction history, is recorded on a blockchain, making it permanently accessible for verification.

- **Programmability**: As with other digital assets on the blockchain, NFTs can incorporate smart contracts that may enable functionalities such as royalties for creators on subsequent sales.

NFTs have gained significant attention for their use in the digital art world, where they are used to buy, sell, and trade digital art, but they also have applications in other areas such as virtual real estate, gaming, and collectibles. The technology opens up new possibilities for digital rights management and ownership in the digital space.

Virtual real estate

Virtual real estate refers to the ownership of virtual land or properties within online worlds, games, or **virtual reality** (**VR**) platforms. These digital assets are often bought, sold, and traded like physical real estate, using real money or cryptocurrencies, and can be developed or customized by their owners for various uses, such as hosting virtual events, creating digital storefronts, or personal or commercial spaces within virtual environments.

Now that you have a grasp of what an NFT is, let's shift our focus to the creative process. Understanding the technology is just the beginning; next, we'll explore how you can leverage this powerful tool to create your own unique NFTs, turning your digital creations into verifiable and tradable assets on the blockchain.

Creating an NFT

Creating visual art for NFTs requires a blend of artistic creativity and an understanding of what resonates in the digital art market. While there's no one-size-fits-all formula for success, certain elements often contribute to the appeal and value of NFT art:

- **Originality and uniqueness**: The most successful NFT art often features a high degree of originality. Unique concepts or distinctive styles stand out in the market. Authenticity in your creative expression can make your NFT more desirable. For example, BAYC stands out as a remarkable NFT collection, renowned for its originality and uniqueness. Each NFT features a distinct monkey character, differentiated by its own set of characteristics. Ownership of one of these NFTs not only signifies holding a unique piece of digital art but also grants exclusive access to a variety of physical perks.

- **Storytelling or conceptual depth**: Art that tells a story or has a deeper conceptual meaning can create a stronger emotional connection with the audience. NFTs that embody a narrative or convey a strong message often garner more interest.

- **Aesthetic appeal**: The visual appeal of the artwork is crucial. This includes factors such as composition, color, texture, and overall visual impact. Aesthetically pleasing artworks tend to attract more viewers and potential buyers.

- **Quality of execution**: High-quality artwork, both in terms of technical execution and artistic merit, is key. This includes attention to detail, skillful use of the medium, and overall professionalism in the presentation of the NFT.

- **Community and social engagement**: In the NFT space, community support can significantly boost the value of an artwork. Artists who engage with their audience through social media or NFT platforms can build a loyal following that values their work.

- **Scarcity and editions**: Limited editions or one-of-a-kind pieces can increase desirability due to their scarcity. However, how you manage editions—whether you create single editions or multiple copies—can also impact value and demand.

- **Interactivity and utility**: Some NFT artworks offer interactive elements or additional utility, such as access to events, physical counterparts, or integration in virtual worlds, which can add value and interest.

- **Artist's reputation and history**: Established artists or those with a growing reputation in the NFT space can command higher prices and interest. The artist's story and background can also play a role in the artwork's value.

- **Technology and innovation**: Utilizing innovative techniques, such as **augmented reality** (**AR**) and VR integration, AI-generated art, or unique digital mediums, can make NFTs stand out.

- **Market trends and timing**: Awareness of current trends in the NFT market, such as popular themes, styles, or types of artworks, can influence the success of an NFT. Timing releases to coincide with high-interest periods can also be beneficial.

Ultimately, the best visual art for NFTs is subjective and varies based on the preferences of collectors and the dynamics of the NFT marketplace. Balancing artistic integrity with market trends and audience preferences is key.

Creating collections

We are going to use Bing Image Creator for this project because it enables us to save our images in collections to better organize our work. Before we create our collections, we must have a clear idea of what we want to create. Let's understand with the help of an example.

Say you come up with an idea to use **Plastic Oceans and Marine Life** as a collection. For this, each NFT could depict a different marine species entangled in or surrounded by plastics, highlighting the threat of pollution to their survival. This series can include animals such as sea turtles, seals, and various species of fish and whales.

Let's consider another example—**Urban Wildlife in a Plastic World**. In this case, you can showcase endangered animals in urban settings, interacting with plastic waste. This could highlight how human urbanization and waste affect wildlife. You could generate images of birds building nests from plastic items, or urban foxes rummaging through plastic waste. Each image you create would have the potential to be transformed into an NFT.

You can also try to create an interactive premise for your NFT. Consider the **Interactive Endangered Species Map** example—an interactive map showing different regions of the world, each highlighting an endangered animal affected by plastic pollution in that area. Clicking on each region could reveal a unique NFT artwork of the animal and information about the environmental challenges it faces. This website will serve as an interactive platform where all your NFTs are showcased and accessible.

In creating these NFTs, it would be important to strike a balance between artistic expression and the delivery of a powerful environmental message. Additionally, you might consider donating a portion of the proceeds from your NFT sales to wildlife conservation or environmental cleanup efforts, further emphasizing the purpose behind your collection.

The transformation of an artwork/image into an official NFT occurs when it is listed on a platform such as OpenSea, which facilitates its integration into the blockchain and links it to a cryptocurrency framework.

Let's walk through how to create these NFTs. We're going to start with these image prompts:

- **Sea Turtle Amidst Plastic Debris**: "Create an image of a sea turtle swimming in clear ocean water, entangled in a variety of colorful plastic bags and bottles. The turtle's expression should convey distress, emphasizing the impact of pollution on marine life. The background should be a mix of coral reefs and open ocean, showcasing the turtle's natural habitat juxtaposed with the invasive plastics." *See Figure 5.1*:

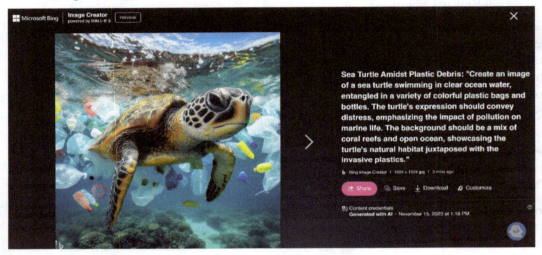

Figure 5.1: DALL-E 3-generated image for NFT

- **Seal in a Plastic-Littered Environment**: "Illustrate a seal lying on a rocky shore, with its surroundings cluttered with plastic waste, including soda rings, straws, and discarded packaging. The seal should appear forlorn and trapped, highlighting the effect of human waste on its habitat. The scene should include a glimpse of the ocean in the background, contrasting the natural beauty of the sea with the harsh reality of pollution."

- **Fish Swimming Through Plastic Rings**: "Generate an image of a group of colorful reef fish swimming through an underwater landscape dominated by discarded plastic six-pack rings and other plastic debris. The fish should appear to be navigating through the obstacles of waste, emphasizing the challenges faced by marine life due to human pollution."

- **Whale Entangled in Fishing Nets and Plastics**: `"Depict a majestic whale entangled in a mix of fishing nets and various plastic items like bags and containers. The whale should be partially submerged in the ocean, with the sun setting in the background, creating a poignant contrast between the beauty of the marine environment and the grim reality of pollution."`

Now, we'll go through two simple steps to save our images and add them to our collection:

1. Click the **Save** button on the right side of the image.

2. Then, click the **Create a new collection** option and name your collection:

Figure 5.2: Saving your image into a collection on Bing Image Creator

Saving your images in a collection, as in *Figure 5.2*, will make it easier when you come back to retrieve those images when you're ready to upload them on your NFT marketplace.

Having covered the creation of collections, we'll now dive into NFT platforms. This will give us insights into how to upload your artwork and convert it into a purchasable NFT.

Exploring NFT platforms

An NFT platform is a digital marketplace or service where users can create, buy, sell, and trade NFTs. As we've discussed, NFTs are unique digital assets verified using blockchain technology; this ensures their authenticity and ownership. NFT platforms play a critical role in the NFT ecosystem, providing a space for artists, creators, and collectors to interact. Here's a breakdown of key aspects of an NFT platform:

- **Blockchain technology**: NFT platforms are built on blockchain technology, primarily Ethereum. The blockchain records all transactions, making them transparent and secure.

- **Minting NFTs**: Creators can "mint" digital items as NFTs on these platforms. Minting means creating a digital record of the artwork or item on the blockchain, thus turning it into a token that can be bought, sold, or traded.

- **Marketplace**: Most NFT platforms feature a marketplace where users can browse, buy, and sell NFTs. These marketplaces display NFTs in various formats, such as digital art, music, videos, and more.

- **Wallets and transactions**: To use an NFT platform, users need a digital wallet compatible with the blockchain the platform operates on. Wallets are used to store NFTs and cryptocurrencies, which are the primary means of transacting on these platforms.

- **Smart contracts**: NFTs are governed by smart contracts, which are self-executing contracts with the terms of the agreement directly written into code. These contracts can automate the distribution of earnings among collaborators on a project whenever the NFT is sold, or even grant holders special access to exclusive online content or real-world events. Additionally, smart contracts can enforce digital scarcity by limiting the number of copies of an NFT that can exist, further enhancing its value and uniqueness.

- **Royalties and earnings**: Artists and creators can earn royalties from their NFTs. When an NFT is resold, a percentage of the sale price can automatically go to the original creator, as defined in the smart contract.

- **Community and social features**: Many NFT platforms incorporate social aspects, allowing users to follow artists, participate in forums, and join virtual events.

- **Variety of NFTs**: These platforms support a wide range of NFTs, including digital art, collectibles, gaming items, virtual real estate, and more.

- **Exclusivity and scarcity**: NFTs often come with a sense of exclusivity or scarcity, which can drive their value. Limited editions or unique items are particularly sought after.

- **Accessibility and user experience**: Good NFT platforms focus on user-friendly interfaces and accessibility, making it easy for both seasoned traders and newcomers to navigate the platform.

Overall, NFT platforms serve as a crucial hub for the world of digital collectibles and assets, offering a unique blend of technology, art, and commerce. We are going to use OpenSea because it is currently the most popular and user-friendly NFT platform. If you already have an account, you can hop right in! If not, you will need to set up an account and connect your digital crypto wallet. First, we'll get you set up with your wallet.

Setting up your wallet

For instructions to set up your wallet, follow these simple steps:

1. Choose a crypto wallet platform. For this chapter, I'm using Coinbase. Use this link to earn up to 40 USD in rewards: `https://packt.link/QG27R`.

2. Create your account. Enter your personal information and choose a secure password. It's also recommended to use **two-step verification** (also called **2FA**) for an extra layer of security. See *Figure 5.3*.

Now, you'll need to buy **ETH (Ethereum)**, because this is the cryptocurrency that backs NFTs. Most crypto platforms and exchanges allow you to buy crypto using a bank account or credit card. I'd recommend around the equivalent of 100 USD to start. This should cover your smart contract.

> **Disclaimer**
> Keep in mind that this market is unpredictable, and it's wise to invest only what you're comfortable potentially losing.

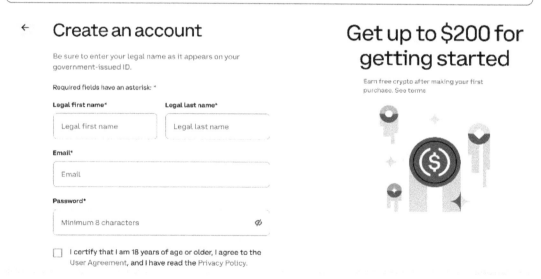

Figure 5.3: Creating your Coinbase account

Now that you have your wallet set up, we can go over to OpenSea and set up your account on the platform.

Opening an NFT account

Opening an account on OpenSea involves a few straightforward steps. Here's a general guide on how to do it:

1. **Visit OpenSea**: Go to the OpenSea website at `opensea.io`.

2. **Connect your wallet**: On the OpenSea website, look for the option to connect your wallet. This is usually a prominent button on the top-right corner of the website. Click on it and choose your wallet from the list of options, as shown in *Figure 5.4*. You'll then be prompted to approve the connection in your wallet:

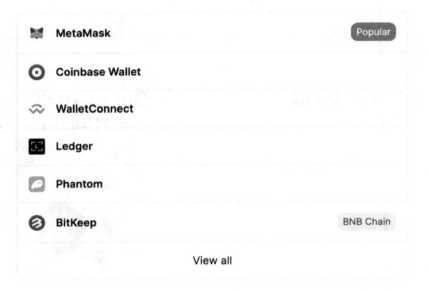

Figure 5.4: Connecting your wallet

3. **Create your OpenSea account**: After connecting your wallet, your OpenSea account is automatically created. Your account is essentially your wallet address.

4. **Customize your profile**: Although it is not mandatory, you can customize your OpenSea profile by adding a profile picture, username, and bio. This can be done by going to your profile page on OpenSea and editing the relevant sections.

5. **Secure your account**: Ensure your digital wallet and OpenSea account are secure. This involves not sharing your private keys or recovery phrase with anyone and being cautious about phishing attempts and suspicious links.

Remember—engaging with digital wallets and NFT marketplaces involves some risks, especially related to security. Always make sure to follow best practices for digital security and thoroughly research any platform or technology you plan to use.

Uploading to an NFT platform

Now that you have an OpenSea account, you can start using it right away! Creating an NFT on OpenSea is a straightforward process, but it requires you to have some familiarity with your digital wallet and the Ethereum blockchain. Here's a step-by-step guide:

1. **Prepare your digital asset**: Before you start, ensure you have a digital asset (such as artwork, music, video, and so on) ready to turn into an NFT. This file should be in a format supported by OpenSea (for example, JPG, PNG, GIF, MP3, MP4).

2. **Go to OpenSea**: Navigate to OpenSea and log in by connecting your digital wallet. See *Figure 5.5*:

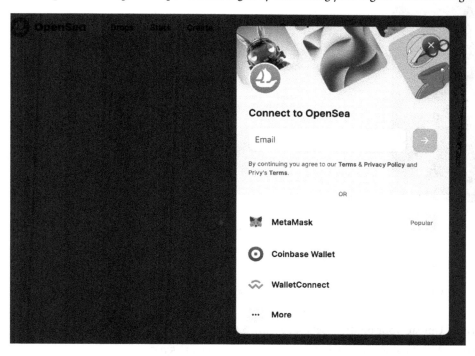

Figure 5.5: OpenSea login screen

3. **Create a collection** (optional but recommended):

   I.   Click on your profile icon and select **My Collections**.

   II. Click on **Create a collection**.

   III. Upload a logo, featured image, and banner for your collection. Fill in details such as name, description, and social links. See *Figure 5.6*.

   IV. Set the royalty percentage, which is the share you'll receive when your NFTs are resold in the secondary market.

   V.   Choose a blockchain for your collection (Ethereum is the most common).

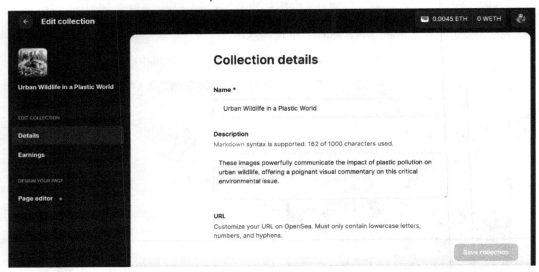

Figure 5.6: Creating a collection in OpenSea

4. **Create a new NFT**:

   I.   Once your collection is set up (or if you're not using a collection), go to your profile icon and select **Create**. See *Figure 5.7*.

   II. Upload your digital asset. See *Figure 5.8*.

   III. Add a name and a detailed description. See *Figure 5.8*.

   IV. You can add properties, levels, and stats if relevant to your NFT.

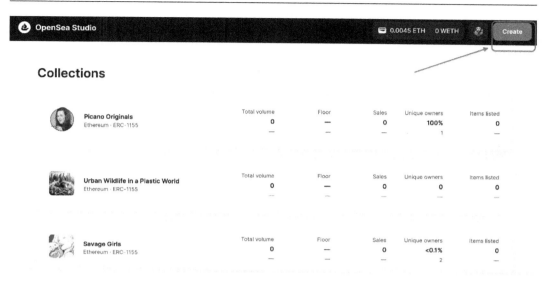

Figure 5.7: Clicking on the Create button to begin your NFT upload

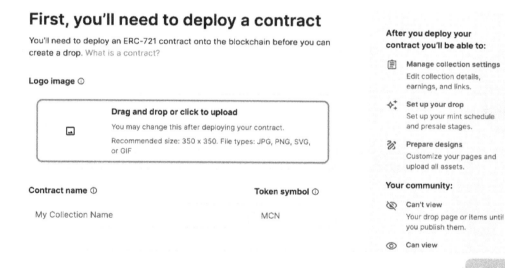

Figure 5.8: Drag and drop your NFT image here

5. **Set up sales options:**

    I. Choose whether to sell your NFT at a fixed price, create a timed auction, or start an unlimited auction.

    II. While setting a price, input the amount and select a cryptocurrency (for example, ETH).

    III. You can also include unlockable content, only visible to the buyer.

6. **Mint your NFT:**

    I. Once you're satisfied with your listing, click **Create** to mint your NFT.

    II. You might be required to sign a transaction in your wallet to approve this action. Note that gas fees (transaction fees on the Ethereum network) may apply, depending on how OpenSea is set up at the time.

7. **List for sale:** After minting your NFT, you can list it for sale. This might require an additional transaction, especially if it's your first time selling on OpenSea.

8. **Manage your listing:** After listing, you can manage your NFT through your profile. You can adjust the price, end or modify the sale, or view bids.

Note

Gas fees: Creating and selling NFTs on the Ethereum blockchain typically involves gas fees, which can vary based on network congestion.

Digital rights: Ensure you have the rights to the content you're turning into an NFT.

Security: Keep your wallet and private keys secure and be wary of phishing attempts.

Now that you know how to create NFTs and organize them into collections, you can choose to drop your collection. To "drop" a collection simply means to release a collection for purchase on the blockchain for the first time. Here are the steps to drop your NFT:

1. First, you need to deploy your contract. To do this, you'll first upload your image by simply dragging and dropping it, as in *Figure 5.8*.

2. Next, give your contract a title, selecting any name that you feel best captures the essence of your artwork.

3. Click the **Continue** button to connect your wallet and release your NFT to the world!

Important

The NFT space is constantly evolving, so it's crucial to stay updated with the latest trends and guidelines. Also, be aware of the legal and tax implications of trading NFTs in your jurisdiction.

Summary

In this chapter, we learned the process of creating an NFT. We discovered how to set up a cryptocurrency wallet and list our NFTs on a platform to make them accessible in the marketplace.

Armed with this knowledge, you're now equipped to launch your own NFT collection or help others in releasing theirs. Moving forward, the next chapter will delve into the art of designing covers for books, magazines, and various publications.

6

Designing Art for Covers of Books, Magazines, and Other Publications

So far, we've seen that in the ever-evolving world of digital art and design, the advent of AI-powered tools such as **DALL-E 3** has marked a revolutionary shift in how we create and conceptualize visuals. In the last chapter, we saw the practical use of AI-generated artwork in the form of NFTs. Now, we'll delve into another interesting and practical application of art generated by DALL-E 3.

In this chapter, we'll explore the practical applications of DALL-E 3 for designing art for book covers, magazines, and other publications, offering tips and strategies for crafting compelling textual prompts that can be translated into stunning visual illustrations. Whether you're looking to create an eye-catching book cover that tells the genre and setting of a story at a glance, a magazine cover that stands out on a newsstand, or any other publication artwork, these pro tips will provide an innovative way to make your creative aspirations a reality.

We're going to cover these aspects under the following main topics:

- Points to consider while creating powerful cover art
- Understanding parameters and sizing
- Altering our prompt to generate a better book cover

Technical requirements

In this chapter, you'll continue to use DALL-E 3 through OpenAI or Bing Image Creator as done in earlier chapters.

You can also use your choice of software to edit your DALL-E 3 generated covers or illustrations if needed. We recommend the following:

- **Canva**: Canva's simplicity and ease of use make it an ideal choice for beginners. It is available at the following link: `https://www.canva.com/`.
- **Adobe Photoshop**: Photoshop's advanced capabilities and industry-standard status make it a preferred option for more experienced designers. It can be accessed here: `https://www.adobe.com/`.

Creating powerful cover art

Creating powerful cover art for your book or magazine is a crucial step in attracting readers and effectively conveying the essence of your work. Here are some steps and tips to guide you through the process:

- **Understand your book or magazine's core theme and audience**: Your cover should instantly give readers a taste of your book's story or your magazine's content. Keep in mind what your audience likes—this will help grab their attention and get them excited about what's inside.
- **Research and gather inspiration**: Check out what's working for bestsellers in your genre — their covers can spark some great ideas. Gather a mix of visuals, colors, and styles that click with what your book or magazine is all about.
- **Choose a focal point**: Choose a standout feature for your cover, such as a bold image or eye-catching text. Make sure it gels with your book's vibe and grabs readers right off the bat.
- **Typography matters**: Pick fonts that match the feel of your content and ensure they're clear enough to read at a glance. Your book or magazine's title and your name should pop out front and center. Consider *IT* by Stephen King, where the bold, dripping letters of the title evoke a sense of horror. Another example would be the subtle, handwritten typography in *The Art of Balancing Burnout* by Vanessa Autrey, which conveys the calming tone of the book.
- **Color scheme**: Go for colors that hit the right emotional note and suit your story or theme. Remember, the colors you choose can shape how readers view your book or magazine. For a mystery/thriller, we might want to choose dark and moody colors such as deep blues, blacks, and grays with accent colors of blood red or ominous green for a sense of danger. Consider the example of a thriller such as *Gone Girl* by Gillian Flynn, where we see the use of black with an accent of red, or *The Woman in the Window* by A.J. Finn, where we again see a dark background with bright red font.

- If we are working with a science fiction title, we might want to go with futuristic metallic colors such as silver or chrome, with neon accents for a high-tech feel. Consider the example of *Neuromancer* by William Gibson.

- Self-help books are more suited to a minimalistic cover with soothing colors and a handwritten type of font. Consider the example of *The Mindfulness Journal* by Corinne Sweet, which has a blue cover, as blue is widely known as a very soothing color that helps calm your mind.

- **Keep it simple and balanced**: Keep it simple and uncluttered for a stronger impact. Make sure the elements on your cover are balanced to avoid it looking too busy.

- **Consider the back cover and spine**: For print editions, ensure the back cover and spine are in sync with the front design. The back should feature a catchy blurb, your bio, and a barcode, all blending seamlessly with the overall look.

- **Test your design**: Get a group from your target audience to look at your draft. Listen to their feedback and be ready to tweak your design based on their input.

- **Software tools**: Use graphic design software such as Adobe Photoshop or Adobe InDesign, or free tools such as Canva to finish your cover.

- **Final review**: Ensure the cover reflects the essence of your book and double-check for any typographic or design errors.

Your book cover is more than just an artistic element; it's a crucial promotional tool that significantly influences your book's market appeal. It's the first indicator of your book's genre, setting expectations right from the start. Think about how fantasy novels often have mystical and otherworldly designs on their covers, instantly attracting fans of the genre. This visual cue is vital for marketing; studies have shown that some book covers can dramatically outperform others in sales, with differences as stark as a 30% increase in clicks and subsequent purchases. This statistic underscores the cover's role as a magnet for potential readers, making it clear that a well-thought-out and targeted cover design isn't just about aesthetics – it's a strategic marketing move that can directly impact your book's success. Let's dig into an example. I'll opt to use DALL-E 3 in OpenAI for creating this book cover, as it appears to be more responsive than Bing Image Creator when adjusting the size of my image. This adjustment is necessary for aligning with the dimensions required for a book cover.

The prompt I put into DALL-E 3 is as follows: `Create a sword with morning glories growing around it in a forest in the morning light, with text at the top "Morning Glory"`.

Figure 6.1: First book cover image example

In *Figure 6.1*, we can see the following:

- **The image is square**: At this time, the default image is square, so we're going to change that.

- **The text appears at the bottom**: In the prompt, we asked for the text "Morning Glory" to be at the top of the image but in the generated image, it appears at the bottom.

- **The title "Morning Glory" is misspelled**: **Misspellings** happen a lot with generative AI. In DALL-E 3-generated images, misspellings can occur for a few reasons:

  - **Training data limitations**: DALL-E 3, like other AI models, is trained on vast datasets of text and images. If the training data contains misspelled words or textual anomalies, these can be inadvertently learned and reproduced by the AI.

  - **Contextual understanding**: AI models may sometimes struggle with the context and nuanced meanings of words, leading to incorrect usage or misspellings, especially with words that sound alike but are spelled differently (homophones).

  - **Complex language rules**: English, with its complex rules and exceptions, can be challenging for AI models. Subtleties in grammar, spelling, and usage can sometimes lead to errors in text generation.

- **Technical limitations**: The algorithms that govern how DALL-E 3 interprets and generates text might not always correctly predict or replicate the correct spelling of all words, especially if they are less common or have multiple spellings.

- **User input**: Sometimes, the misspellings could be a result of the input provided to DALL-E 3. If the user's request contains misspellings, these will likely be reflected in the output.

It's important to remember that AI, including DALL-E 3, is constantly evolving, and improvements in natural language processing and image generation are continuously being made to reduce such errors. This is why we're going to use one of the programs mentioned earlier in the *Technical requirements* section for the finishing touches.

We will regenerate this image with two changes in the prompt:

- We will not include the title in the visual design. Instead, we'll add the title afterward using a separate process.

- For the regeneration, we'll specify the image size in the prompt to ensure it aligns well with the dimensions of a book cover.

First, I'll take you through the industry standards for book parameters and sizing, then we'll revisit this cover to make the iterations.

Parameters and sizing

Let's talk about the industry standards for book cover designs. Here's a breakdown of common terms and standards:

- **File type**: If you are submitting a book cover file to an online print-on-demand service, you'll want to choose the correct file type. Note that the default option for saving DALL-E 3 images is WebP on OpenAI and JPG on Bing (at the time of writing). You can read more about print-on-demand services here: https://www.oberlo.com/blog/print-on-demand-books.

- **Color settings**: You'll want to save your image as an RGB file if your book is online, or a CMYK file if it'll be printed. The choice between RGB and CMYK depends on the final medium where the image will be displayed. RGB is optimal for digital screens due to its ability to represent a wide range of colors through light, while CMYK is essential for printed materials because it aligns with the color-mixing process of physical printing.

- **Resolution**: Use **pixels per inch** (**PPI**) if your cover is designed to be viewed digitally, and **dots per inch** (**DPI**) if your cover will be printed. For most projects, the standard is 72 PPI for web content and 300 DPI for printed materials. To learn about PPI versus DPI, you can read more here: https://vimm.com/dpi-vs-pixels/.

Standard cover sizes

Here, we'll look at standard cover sizes for printed books, e-books, and magazines. We'll be presenting these dimensions in inches for physical copies, while the sizes for digital covers will be indicated in pixels.

Printed book covers

These are the hard or soft physical covers of books, designed to protect the pages while visually representing the book's content and theme. They often include elements such as the title, author, and artwork, and are tactile, offering a distinct texture and weight. Notably, these covers vary in size to align with the book's purpose, from compact handbooks to larger, more elaborate volumes.

Printed book covers	Sizes in inches
Mass market paperback	4.25 x 6.87
Trade paperback	5.5 x 8.5, 6 x 9
Hardcover book	6 x 9 8.5 x 11
Nonfiction book	5.5 x 8.5, 6 x 9, 7 x 10
Novella	5 x 8
Children's book	7.5 x 7.5, 7 x 10 10 x 8
Textbook	6 x 9 7 x 10, 8.5 x 11

Table 6.1: Dimensions of printed book covers

E-book covers

E-book covers are digital representations of traditional book covers, optimized for viewing on electronic devices such as e-readers, tablets, and computers. Sizes are represented in pixels. A pixel aspect ratio is the mathematical ratio defining how a pixel's shape is proportioned in terms of its width and height.

E-book covers	Sizes in pixels (aspect ratio)
Kindle Direct	2,560 x 1,600 (1.6:1)
Novels and non-fiction	2,560 x 1,600 (1.6:1)
Illustrated book	2,800 x 3,920 (1.4:1) or 3,000 x 3,600 (1.2:1)
Audiobook	3,200 x 3,200 (1:1)

Table 6.2: Dimensions of e-book covers

Printed magazine covers

Magazine covers are designed to be eye catching and informative, featuring vivid images, prominent titles, and headlines to entice potential readers. They are typically glossy and visually rich, showcasing the magazine's main themes or featured articles to stand out in a crowded newsstand environment.

Printed magazine covers	Sizes in inches
A4	8.3 x 11.7
Digest	5.5 x 8.25
Half letter	8.5 x 5.5
Letter	8.5 x 11
Tabloid	11 x 17
Broadsheet	22.5 x 35
Square	5.5 x 5.5, 8.5 x 8.5

Table 6.3: Dimensions of printed magazine covers

Having explored the various dimensions of book cover sizes, let's now transition into the next crucial step in the *Choosing the right book or magazine cover size* section. This section will guide you through the factors to consider in selecting the ideal size that not only matches your creative vision but also aligns with industry standards and reader expectations.

Choosing the right book or magazine cover size

Now that you're familiar with the standard dimension choices for physical books, magazines, and e-books, here are some basic factors to consider:

- **Word count**: Take into consideration the word and page counts. It wouldn't be the best idea to choose a large page size for a short novella, or a small size for a lengthy book.

- **Place of sale**: Where will your book be sold? Consider whether your publication is a printed book, e-book, children's book, or another format. If you're working with a large publishing house, these decisions will most likely be made for you, but if you are self-publishing, you will need to figure this out for yourself.

Now that we've covered the basics of sizing and parameters for different book and magazine covers, let's circle back to our earlier example for a more detailed exploration.

Altering our prompt to generate a better book cover

Recall that the cover we created earlier encountered some problems, including incorrect cover size, misspelled title, and improper placement of the title text. Let's look into how we can address and rectify these issues.

We can alter our initial prompt to remove the text "Morning Glory" by simply not including it in the next prompt, and include the output size of 1,024 x 1,792. See our following updated prompt:

```
Create morning glories crawling around a sword in the forest with
morning sunlight coming through the trees, 1024x1792.
```

As you can observe, in this prompt I am telling DALL-E 3 that I need a vertical image when I end my prompt with `1024x1792`. Note that when you use size prompts, the first figure is the width, followed by the height. See *Figure 6.2*.

Figure 6.2: Add the 1024x1792 size parameter

At times, the specific dimensions you request in your prompt might not be correctly processed, especially if an incorrect size is used. This happens because DALL-E 3 is programmed to recognize only three specific sizes: 1,024px x 1,024px, 1,792px x 1,024px, and 1,024px x 1,792px. In such scenarios, it's advisable to resubmit your prompt with one of these exact dimensions. If the resulting image still isn't quite what you had in mind, remember to refine your prompts using the techniques we explored in *Chapter 2*. This approach will help you gradually achieve an image that closely matches your original vision.

> **Note**
>
> Modifying existing book covers without permission could result in copyright infringement. The example here creates an original cover design for illustrative purposes.

As discussed earlier, I'll be using Canva to design our cover, because it's fast and user friendly. Canva suits beginners well, but if your publisher specifies the need for an **Encapsulated PostScript** (**EPS**) or **Scalable Vector Graphics** (**SVG**) file, you might have to opt for more sophisticated software such as Adobe Illustrator.

Here are the steps you'll take to finalize the book cover by adding details if you're using Canva:

1. Navigate to `https://www.canva.com/`.
2. Use the search bar to find book cover templates. See *Figure 6.3*.

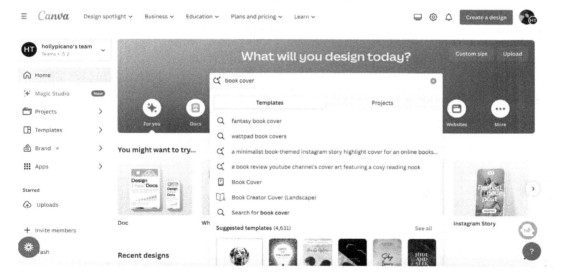

Figure 6.3: Canva interface

3. Choose a template that most aligns with your vision. If you don't find one that resonates with you, don't worry; you can change all of the elements within the template to suit your needs.
4. Click on **Customize this template**. See *Figure 6.4*.

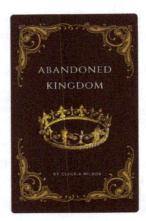

Brown and Orange Elegant Simple Young Adult Fantasy Book Cover

Book Cover • 1410 × 2250 px

By Nasiyat Akmatova

Customize this template

100% fully customizable

Edit and download on the go

Share and publish anywhere

Figure 6.4: Canva book cover template example

5.   This action opens up possibilities for modifications, allowing you to alter text, choose various font styles and colors, and even change the background image.

6.   As you proceed to customize your book cover, the next step is to upload your image file. To do this, click on the **Upload files** button, and select the image files you wish to upload – these images will then be displayed on the left side of the screen. Following that, we'll drag and drop the selected image into our template, as demonstrated in *Figure 6.5*.

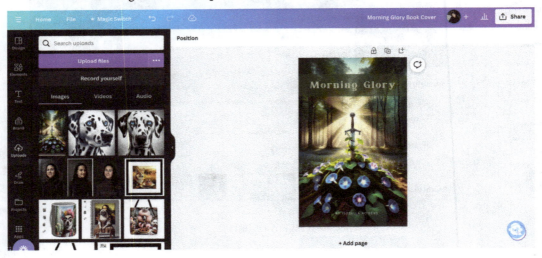

Figure 6.5: Edit template and upload files

7. Here, we are changing the title to "Morning Glory" by simply clicking into the original text and editing it directly. Now, we can make our font style and color choices.

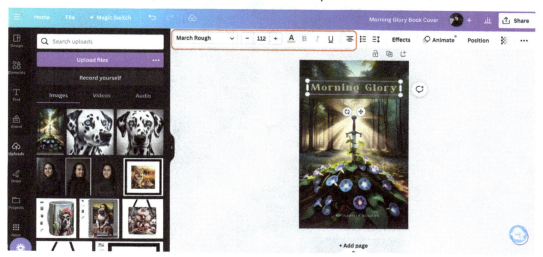

Figure 6.6: Font style and color choices

8. When you click on the text box, you'll see options for font style, size, color, and so on at the top of the screen, as shown in *Figure 6.6*. In this instance, we've selected the `March Rough` font style, increased the font size to `112`, and a font color with the `#D1CCAB` hex code. *Figure 6.7* showcases the completed book cover.

Figure 6.7: Final book cover

We ensured that the design not only captured the essence of your book but also adhered to the necessary technical specifications for publishing. We looked into fine-tuning elements such as layout, typography, and color schemes. We also discussed how to prepare your cover for the final submission, whether it was for digital or print publication. We moved forward together to bring our vision to life and made our book cover stand out in the crowded world of publishing. Next, we'll look at saving your final project as a file, ready to send and share with the world.

> **Note**
>
> Upon downloading your image in OpenAI, DALL-E 3 saves your image as a WebP file. To save your image as a JPEG or PNG, simply open your file. On a Mac, your file will open in Preview. Then, click on File > Export > and click on the toggle for file type and choose JPG or PNG. PNG is advised for maintaining the image quality of the final book cover. For needs involving CMYK or other file formats, employ photo editing software to convert the files after downloading. Ensure to save a master copy in the PNG format before any conversions.

Presenting our finished book cover

Having completed our book cover, it's now time to present it to our boss, client, or anyone else who needs to review it! These are the steps we'll take to prepare our image:

1. Click on the **Share** button at the top-right side of the page.

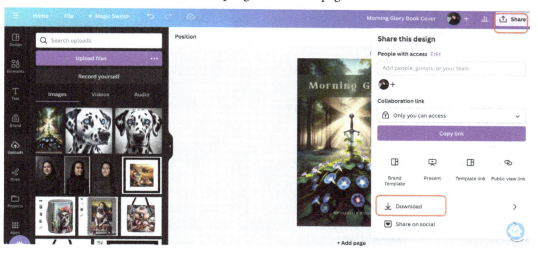

Figure 6.8: Initiate the download

2. Click on **Download**.
3. You'll encounter various file type options. Select what type of file you want to save your cover as (JPG, PNG, or PDF).

4. To access a broader range of file types, click on the down arrow next to the file type. This will reveal a drop-down menu with additional options, as illustrated in *Figure 6.9*.

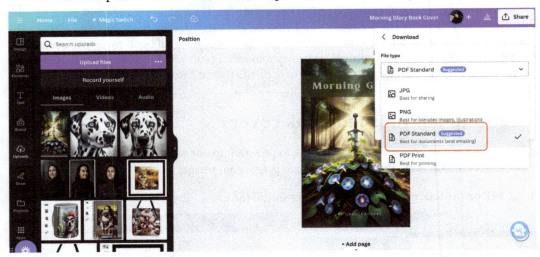

Figure 6.9: Select the file type to download

With your file now ready, you can proceed to print it or share it through email, text message, or on social media platforms.

Summary

This chapter explored the crucial steps needed to attract the right audience with compelling cover art and illustrations. We delved into the standard sizes for book and magazine covers and outlined how to craft artwork that adheres to these sizes, using precise prompts to adjust the image dimensions. We also covered how to save the final cover image in different formats.

Now that we've explored the practical use of AI-generated art in book and magazine covers, we now turn our attention to the future possibilities of AI in the realm of art.

Part 3:
The Future of AI and Art

In this section, we look at the intricate skill of formulating captivating prompts for diverse purposes. A comprehensive cheat sheet becomes your quick reference guide, presenting techniques that make prompts impactful and result-driven.

This part has the following chapters:

- *Chapter 7, Exploring the Ethical Dimensions and the Future of Art*
- *Chapter 8, Effective Prompt Cheat Sheet*
- *Chapter 9, Case Studies, Interviews, and Insights*

7

Exploring the Ethical Dimensions and the Future of Art

In this chapter, we look into the critical considerations surrounding the ethical use of AI in art creation and the prospective future of this intersection between technology and creativity. You will be guided through the topics of intellectual property rights, originality, machine bias, and the responsible use of AI. It's vital to look at AI from an ethical standpoint because it helps us navigate the complex moral landscape of creativity and technology, ensuring that we respect the rights and contributions of artists while fostering innovation and fairness in this rapidly evolving field. This approach not only safeguards artistic integrity but also builds public trust in the use of AI.

By the end of this chapter, you will come away with a well-rounded understanding of the current state and potential future of AI in the art world, especially focusing on the legal, ethical, and societal implications. You will be equipped with knowledge about both the opportunities and challenges presented by AI tools, such as DALL-E 3, in the creative process.

We'll be covering the following main topics:

- Intellectual property rights and originality
- Machine bias and how to control it
- The future of AI art

Intellectual property rights and originality

As we examine the fascinating realm of AI-generated art with DALL-E 3, it's crucial for us to understand the intricacies of **intellectual property (IP)** rights. Intellectual property is a term that refers to creations of the mind, such as inventions, literary and artistic works, designs, symbols, names, and images used in commerce. Essentially, it's a way of legally protecting these creations. The owner of an IP can control and receive financial benefits from their work, preventing others from using it without permission. It's like having a legal claim over your unique ideas or creations, ensuring that the original creator gets credit and any financial rewards that come from their work.

When diving into the world of AI-generated art, especially with tools such as DALL-E 3, we encounter a series of intriguing challenges related to IP. These challenges revolve around key aspects that redefine our understanding of creativity and ownership in the digital age. Let's explore these aspects in more detail:

- **Authorship and ownership**: Traditionally, IP rights are granted to human creators. However, in the case of DALL-E 3, we are faced with the basic question: who is the creator? Is it the developers who designed the AI, the users who input prompts, or the AI itself? Current legal frameworks generally don't recognize AI as an independent creator, which leads us to a fascinating conundrum. We, as users of DALL-E 3, might be seen as the authors since we provide the creative input that the AI transforms into art. However, the significant role of AI in shaping the final artwork cannot be overlooked.

- **Originality of art**: DALL-E 3 creates images based on a vast database of pre-existing artworks and visual information. This raises questions about the originality of the output. Can AI-generated art be considered truly original if it's derived from pre-existing works? We find ourselves navigating the thin line between inspiration and infringement, a line that's even more blurred in the digital age.

Back in January 2023, artists Sarah Andersen, Kelly McKernan, and Karla Ortiz took a big step by suing Stability AI, Midjourney, and DeviantArt. They argued that these companies wrongfully used over five billion images, including their work, to train AI without asking the artists first. That same month, Getty Images also sued Stability AI, accusing them of using their images for AI training without permission. You can read more about these issues here:

- *In a Blow for Artists, a Federal Judge Has Sided With Three A.I. Companies in a Copyright Dispute*: `https://news.artnet.com/art-world/federal-judge-sides-with-ai-companies-in-artists-copyright-dispute-2387654`

- *Getty Images lawsuit says Stability AI misused photos to train AI*: `https://www.reuters.com/legal/getty-images-lawsuit-says-stability-ai-misused-photos-train-ai-2023-02-06/`

Fast forward to July 2023, and the situation took a turn. US District Judge William Orrick was leaning toward dismissing most of the claims made by Andersen, McKernan, and Ortiz. However, he did give them a chance to come back with a revised complaint (read here: *AI-generated art cannot be copyrighted, rules a US federal judge*, `https://www.theverge.com/2023/8/19/23838458/ai-generated-art-no-copyright-district-court`).

- **Copyright infringement**: When AI recreates styles or elements from copyrighted works, as enthusiasts of AI art, we must be vigilant about the sources our AI tools are trained on and the potential for inadvertently reproducing copyrighted material.

As we explore this landscape, we must consider the evolving nature of IP laws. Laws are adapting, albeit slowly, to the new realities brought about by AI in creative fields. We're witnessing a legal transformation, one that will redefine the boundaries of creativity, ownership, and artistic expression.

In April 2023, a groundbreaking decision from a federal court in Washington, D.C., declared that art made by AI doesn't get the same copyright protection as art made by humans. This ruling, made by US District Judge Beryl Howell, might signal trickier cases ahead as AI keeps shaking up the world of creative arts. The origin of AI-generated art has led to the rethinking of traditional notions of authorship, originality, and artistic creation in the age of AI.

Now that we've explored the parallels between AI as a tool in art creation and the traditional role of art supplies, let's shift our focus to the pivotal question at the heart of this discussion: who actually holds creative ownership over content generated by AI? This topic not only dives into the legal intricacies of copyright laws but also touches upon the evolving relationship between human creativity and technological innovation.

Who is the creator?

In our exploration of creative ownership in the complex world of AI-generated art with DALL-E 3, we find ourselves grappling with a fundamental question: who is the creator? As we discussed earlier, this question is pivotal, as it touches on the very essence of intellectual property rights and artistic authorship.

Let's consider the various entities involved in the process:

- **Developers**: Initially, we might think of the developers of DALL-E 3 as the creators. After all, they are the ones who have engineered the AI, setting the foundation for its creative outputs. They have programmed the algorithms and fed the system with a vast array of data, enabling it to generate art. However, their role is more akin to that of facilitators, as they do not directly create the artwork that DALL-E 3 produces. Just as canvases and paints are tools used by an artist to create a work of art, AI can be seen as a tool used by a human creator. The seller of art supplies (which is akin to the AI platform) provides the means for creation but is not the creator. Similarly, AI generates art based on input, but it's humans who guide this process and make creative decisions.

- **AI itself (in this case, DALL-E 3)**: Then, there's the AI. DALL-E 3 processes inputs and generates art, making it seem like a creator. Yet, current legal frameworks do not recognize AI as an independent entity capable of holding copyrights. The AI's role is more of a tool or medium, as we mentioned earlier, like a brush in a painter's hand, albeit a highly sophisticated one.

- **Users**: This leads us to consider ourselves, the users, as the potential creators. When we use DALL-E 3, we input prompts or parameters based on our creative vision. The AI then generates artwork based on these inputs. In this sense, we are directing the creative process, making us akin to the directors of the artwork. Our input is crucial in shaping the final outcome, even though the actual "hand" creating the art is the AI.

In our current legal and societal framework, we, the users, are most closely aligned with the role of the creator when it comes to AI-generated art. We provide the creative direction and input, even though the actual creation process is carried out by the AI. However, as technology and laws evolve, our understanding of authorship and creativity in the context of AI-generated art may undergo significant shifts. For now, in the case of DALL-E 3, it's a collaborative dance between human intention and AI capabilities, with us, the users, leading the way.

Having touched on the complex issue of creative ownership in AI-generated content, let's now turn our attention to another equally intriguing question: can AI-generated art truly be considered original? This section will explore the depths of originality in the realm of AI creativity, challenging our traditional understanding of what it means for a work of art to be truly unique and novel.

Can AI-generated art truly be considered original?

We discussed how DALL-E 3 was trained in *Chapter 1* and how its learning process heavily relies on existing artworks and visual data. This background is crucial as it sets the stage for a thought-provoking question we now face: can AI-generated art be considered truly original if it's derived from pre-existing works? This inquiry is central to our understanding of creativity and originality in the age of advanced technology.

AI tools such as DALL-E 3 operate by analyzing and learning from a vast array of existing artworks and visual inputs. They understand styles, patterns, and elements from these sources, using this knowledge to create something that appears new. However, the fact that these AI-generated creations are fundamentally based on pre-existing works compels us to question the originality of the output. Is it possible for a piece to be truly original if it is essentially an amalgamation and reinterpretation of existing material? This section delves into these complexities, challenging our conventional notions of creativity in the digital era.

The way in which DALL-E 3 interprets our prompts and generates art is often unpredictable and can result in unique combinations and interpretations that no human artist might conceive. This unpredictability and the novel way in which AI combines elements could be argued to result in original creations.

Let's look at the process of creating art from an alternate perspective. Just like how human artists pick up various techniques, get inspired by different styles, and draw influence from the art they've seen, we still see their creations as original. Take the example of Pablo Picasso and Henri Matisse, two iconic artists of their time, who shared a remarkable friendship and artistic journey. They often painted together and were deeply influenced by each other's work. This camaraderie and mutual influence was common among artists of that era. They would exchange ideas, challenge each other's techniques, and draw inspiration from one another's styles. This interaction didn't diminish the originality of their work; rather, it enriched their individual artistic expressions, leading to some of the most celebrated art pieces in history. Their relationship is a testament to how artists grow and evolve through collaboration and shared influences. So, one might argue that AI-generated art simply follows a similar path of inspiration and reinterpretation but in a more advanced and technologically driven manner.

As we consider the originality of AI-generated art, we find ourselves navigating a complex landscape where technology, creativity, and legal definitions intersect. While current legal and artistic frameworks may struggle to categorize the originality of AI art, it's clear that the way we define and understand originality is evolving, just as our artistic tools are.

With this understanding of how artists have historically influenced each other, let's now pivot to a related but more complex issue of copyright infringement in the context of generative AI. This topic takes us into the intricate interplay between technology's capability to create and the legal boundaries that protect original works, a crucial conversation in today's digital and artistically interconnected world.

Copyright infringement and generative AI

As we venture further into the world of generative AI and its artistic capabilities, particularly with tools such as DALL-E 3, we encounter a significant concern of copyright infringement that we, as users and creators, must conscientiously navigate to respect the intellectual property rights of others while exploring the creative potential of AI.

Let's look at an actual case that has recently made headlines.

Case study – Hollie Mengert's Disney illustrations

The issue of whether an AI model's output can be copyrighted depends largely on how much humans are involved in the process. Consider the situation of Hollie Mengert, a Disney illustrator. She discovered that a mechanical engineering student in Canada had used her art style for an AI experiment. The student trained a machine learning model with 32 of Mengert's artworks to replicate her style. Mengert expressed to Andy Baio, who reported the incident, her discomfort with this, saying it felt like a misuse of her work and skills, which she's developed over the years since art school in 2011, without her consent or permission.

Is this fair? And what can Mengert do about it?

To dig deeper into these questions and the legalities around generative AI, *The Verge*, a technology news website headquartered in New York City, consulted various experts, including lawyers, analysts, and AI start-up employees. Some believe these AI systems could indeed violate copyright laws and might face legal challenges soon. Others are just as convinced that everything in the field of generative AI is legally fine, predicting that any lawsuits would likely fail.

Andy Baio, who has been tracking the generative AI scene closely, shared with *The Verge*, "*I see people on both sides of this extremely confident in their positions, but the truth is that nobody really knows. Anyone claiming to know exactly how this will pan out in court is mistaken.*"

Andres Guadamuz, a University of Sussex academic expert in AI and intellectual property law, believes that despite the many uncertainties in this field, a few critical questions lie at the core of the debate. Firstly, is it possible to copyright the output of a generative AI model, and if so, who actually holds that copyright? Secondly, if someone owns the copyright to the data used to train an AI, does that translate to any legal rights over the AI model or its generated content? Answering these questions leads to an even broader one: how do we handle the consequences of this technology? What kinds of legal measures might need to be implemented regarding data collection? And importantly, how can we balance the interests of those developing these AI systems with the rights of individuals whose data is crucial for their operation?

Keeping this framework in mind, it seems probable that most of what generative AI models produce won't be eligible for copyright protection. Typically, these models generate content in large quantities using just a few keywords as prompts. However, cases involving more intricate processes could stand a better chance. Take, for instance, the debated AI-generated artwork that clinched a prize at a state art fair. Here, the creator spent weeks perfecting his prompts and manually tweaking the final artwork, indicating a substantial level of intellectual input.

Giorgio Franceschelli, a computer scientist who has investigated AI copyright issues, points out that assessing human contribution will be particularly crucial in the European Union when it comes to legal decisions. In the UK, which is another key area of focus for Western AI start-ups, the situation differs again. Interestingly, the UK is one of the few countries that offer copyright for works created entirely by a computer. In these cases, the law considers the author to be "*the person by whom the arrangements necessary for the creation of the work are undertaken.*" This definition leaves the interpretation of whether the author is the AI model's developer or the user open. However, it does lay the groundwork for some level of copyright protection.

But securing copyright is just the beginning, warns Andres Guadamuz. He points out that "*The US copyright office is not a court. Registration is needed if you plan to sue for copyright infringement, but ultimately, it's a court that will determine the legal enforceability of that copyright.*"

How can artists and AI companies find common ground?

Even if the use of existing artworks for training generative AI models is deemed fair use, it won't fully address the challenges in this field. This ruling won't satisfy artists upset about their creations being used for commercial AI training, nor does it automatically apply to other areas such as AI-generated code and music. Considering this, we're faced with a critical question: what are the solutions, technical or otherwise, that can be implemented to support the growth of generative AI while also acknowledging and compensating the original creators who have made this field viable?

A straightforward solution might be to license the data and compensate its creators. However, some argue this approach could cripple the industry. Bryan Casey and Mark Lemley, who penned the influential legal paper *Fair Learning* argue that the scale of training datasets for generative AI makes licensing all underlying materials (such as photos, videos, audio files, or texts) impractical for new uses. They believe that accepting any copyright claims could effectively ban the use of such data, not necessarily ensuring compensation for copyright owners. According to them, embracing "fair learning" fosters innovation and contributes to the advancement of superior AI systems rather than restricting their development.

Andy Baio points out a significant challenge: many of those most impacted by AI technology, such as artists, aren't well equipped to engage in legal battles. He notes the following:

> *"They (artists) don't have the resources. Litigation is costly and time-consuming, and you only pursue it if you're confident of winning. That's why I believe the first lawsuits in AI art might come from stock image companies. They're likely to be the biggest losers from this technology, they can easily demonstrate extensive use of their images in training these models, and they have the financial means to afford court proceedings."*

Andres Guadamuz echoes this sentiment. He highlights the daunting expense involved in such legal cases. "*Everyone is aware of the costs,*" he remarks. "*The initial lawsuit will likely lead to a series of appeals, possibly reaching all the way up to the Supreme Court.*" This lengthy legal process emphasizes the challenges facing those who wish to challenge the use of their work in AI technology.

Shutterstock is taking steps to address this issue by planning to establish a fund to pay individuals whose work has been sold to AI companies for model training. Similarly, **DeviantArt** has introduced a metadata tag for images uploaded on the web, signaling AI researchers to avoid scraping these images. **Cohost**, a smaller social network, has adopted this tag site-wide and has stated it might consider legal action if it finds its images being scraped. However, these methods have received varied reactions from the art community. There are lingering questions: can one-off licensing payments truly make up for the potential loss of income for artists? And what about the artists whose work has already been used to train commercial AI systems? How effective are no-scraping tags in such retrospective cases?

As we now know, the challenge arises when the AI, based on its training, produces artwork that closely resembles or replicates elements from copyrighted material. This can lead to potential copyright infringement, a situation where the AI-generated work unlawfully uses the copyrighted material without authorization. We also learned earlier in this chapter that US District Judge Beryl Howell declared that art made by AI doesn't get the same copyright protection as art made by humans. So, what does this mean exactly? The scary truth is that nobody knows what will happen next.

As we continue to explore the use of generative AI in our artistic endeavors, it's crucial to keep these challenges in mind. We need to think carefully about where the AI's training data comes from, what kinds of prompts we're using, and how similar the AI-generated creations might be to existing copyrighted works. Striking the right balance between taking advantage of AI's innovative potential and honoring intellectual property rights at the core of creative fields is key. This mindful approach leads us to our next topic: understanding and addressing machine bias in AI systems.

Machine bias and how to control it

Machine bias occurs when an AI system reflects the prejudices or biases present in its training data. These data often originate from human sources and, consequently, may carry inherent biases related to race, gender, culture, and more. In the context of AI-generated art, this bias can manifest in various ways, such as over-representing certain aesthetics, styles, or subjects while under-representing others.

We believe in the power of community involvement and diverse perspectives in AI development. Including voices from various backgrounds and disciplines can provide a broader, more inclusive view that helps identify and rectify biases that a more homogeneous group might overlook.

As we navigate the world of AI and its applications in creative fields, our awareness and actions toward controlling machine bias are pivotal. It's a responsibility that we carry to ensure that the advancements in AI are not only innovative and powerful but also fair, inclusive, and ethically sound. This journey isn't without its challenges, but it's one that we must undertake with commitment and vigilance.

Controlling machine bias, especially in the context of AI systems such as DALL-E 3, is a multifaceted task that requires a concerted effort from developers, users, and stakeholders. To control and mitigate machine bias, we must first acknowledge and understand its existence and roots. This involves scrutinizing the datasets used for training AI models such as DALL-E 3. Ensuring diversity in training data is a crucial step toward reducing bias.

Here's how we can approach this:

- **Diverse and inclusive training data**: The foundation of controlling machine bias lies in the data used to train AI models. We must ensure that this data is diverse and inclusive, representing a wide range of human experiences, cultures, and perspectives. This helps in reducing the likelihood of the AI system inheriting biases present in more limited or skewed datasets.

- **Regular auditing and bias testing**: Continuously testing AI systems for bias is crucial. This involves regularly auditing the outputs to check for any skewed or prejudiced results. When biases are identified, the model should be adjusted and retrained as necessary. This process should be ongoing to refine the AI's performance continually.

- **Transparent AI algorithms**: Understanding how an AI system makes decisions is key to identifying potential biases. This requires a level of transparency in the AI algorithms. While complete transparency can be challenging due to the complexity of these systems, striving for as much clarity as possible is important.

- **Ethical AI development practices**: Establishing and adhering to ethical guidelines in AI development is essential. This includes considerations of fairness, respect for privacy, and accountability. Developers and companies should commit to ethical AI practices, ensuring that their work prioritizes the reduction of bias.

- **Incorporating feedback loops**: Feedback from users and stakeholders, especially those from diverse backgrounds, is invaluable in identifying and correcting biases. An AI system should be adaptable and capable of learning from feedback to improve its fairness and inclusivity.

- **Interdisciplinary collaboration**: Collaboration between AI developers, ethicists, sociologists, cultural experts, and other relevant stakeholders can provide a more comprehensive approach to identifying and mitigating biases. Diverse perspectives can highlight biases that might not be obvious to those with a more technical focus.

- **Educating AI users**: Users of AI systems should be educated about the potential for bias. Understanding that AI tools are not infallible and can reflect biases helps users to be more critical and mindful of the results they obtain.

- **Legal and regulatory frameworks**: Advocating for and adhering to legal and regulatory standards that govern the ethical use of AI is important. These frameworks can provide guidelines and boundaries for AI development and use, ensuring accountability for biased outcomes.

In summary, controlling machine bias is a dynamic and ongoing process that requires a blend of technical, ethical, and regulatory approaches. It's about creating AI systems that are not only intelligent and capable but are also fair, equitable, and reflective of the diverse world we live in.

Having explored the complexities of controlling machine bias and striving for AI systems that are intelligent, fair, and reflective of our diverse world, we now turn our gaze to the future of AI art.

The future of AI art

As we look towards the future of AI art, which is a future that we are actively shaping, we find ourselves on the cusp of a revolution that is redefining creativity and artistic expression. The integration of AI, particularly in the realm of generative art, is not just a technological advancement; it's a cultural and artistic milestone. Let's consider the future of AI art in a few different aspects:

- **Collaboration**: In the future, we envision AI art becoming more collaborative. Artists and AI will work in tandem, each bringing their unique strengths to the table. The AI's ability to process vast amounts of data and generate complex patterns will complement the human artist's intuition, emotion, and vision. This synergy will give birth to new art forms and styles that are currently unimaginable.

- **Accessibility**: We also foresee AI art becoming more accessible and democratized. With tools such as DALL-E 3, people who may not have formal training in art will be able to express their creativity and produce stunning works. This accessibility could lead to a surge in creativity and diversity in art as people from different backgrounds and cultures contribute their perspectives.

- **Participation**: We anticipate advancements in AI will enable more interactive and immersive art experiences. Imagine art that adapts to the viewer's mood or responses, creating a dynamic and personalized experience. The line between the viewer and the artwork will blur, leading to more engaging and participatory forms of art.

- **Balance**: As AI becomes a more integral part of the art world, we must ensure that it enhances rather than replaces human creativity. It's important to maintain a balance where AI serves as a tool for artistic expression without diminishing the value of human artistry.

- **Education**: In the realm of education and skill development, the rise of AI art will likely influence art education, with new curriculums focusing on the intersection of art and technology. Artists and designers will need to adapt and acquire skills that enable them to harness the power of AI in their creative processes.

The future of AI art is vibrant and full of potential, marked by increased collaboration, accessibility, and innovation. However, with the rise in possibilities, we will also face an increase in ethical and legal concerns; issues of copyright, authorship, and originality will continue to evolve and will require thoughtful consideration and adaptation of laws and norms.

Now, let's look at a few future scenarios.

Use case – Personalized art creation for consumers

AI-generated art is becoming deeply personalized, allowing individuals to create custom artwork based on their preferences, memories, or emotions. Imagine an AI that can craft a painting or digital artwork that reflects your mood based on inputs such as your favorite colors or themes. This technology could also be used in therapeutic settings, helping people express emotions through art when they find it hard to do so with words.

To illustrate the kind of deeply personal artwork we can create, I'd like to share a piece I made for my mother during her illness. Let's apply what we learned in *Chapter 4*, specifically in *Figure 4.1*, by using Fine Art America to upload our image to make it available to place on merchandise. Let's take the example of my mother's Russian Blue cat, Charlie, whom she adores! My mother also has a special fondness for daffodils. With this in mind, I crafted an artwork that merges these beloved elements, as you can see in *Figure 7.1*:

Figure 7.1: Deeply personal AI-generated art

For this unique piece, I had it printed on a coffee mug, allowing my mother to appreciate this special artwork each morning as she sips her coffee (see *Figure 7.2*).

Customized merchandise such as mugs, shirts, and other items has been a popular concept for some time, allowing individuals to imprint chosen designs, photos, or text on various products. However, the development of AI-generated art takes this idea a step further. Now, even those without traditional artistic skills can create unique and personalized artwork. AI technology enables individuals to input their ideas, emotions, or specific design elements, which the AI then interprets to create original art. This custom-made art can then be transferred onto merchandise, offering a new level of personalization. People can share their own creative expressions or meaningful designs with others in a tangible form without the need for conventional artistic abilities. This advancement democratizes art creation, making it accessible and personalized for everyone:

Figure 7.2: AI art on a coffee mug

Now, let's explore a hypothetical case study to better understand a potential future scenario involving generative AI and its interaction with the legal system.

Case study – The "Artificial Painter" – Intellectual property rights and generative AI

The "Artificial Painter" case study I present is fictional, designed to illustrate the complexities and potential legal scenarios involving intellectual property rights and generative AI. It is not based on an actual legal case or real events. However, it draws upon common themes and hypothetical situations that are currently being discussed in the fields of AI, law, and creative arts. The intention in creating this fictional case study is to provide a conceptual understanding of the issues that could arise in this rapidly evolving area.

Background

Let's say this takes place in 2024; a groundbreaking case has emerged centered around "Artificial Painter," a sophisticated AI program developed by a tech start-up named CreativAI (this company is fictional). This program was designed to generate original artworks by analyzing and processing styles from a vast database of classical and contemporary art. A collection of its creations was exhibited at a renowned art gallery, receiving both critical acclaim and public interest. However, the exhibit sparked a legal debate when several artists claimed that specific pieces bore striking resemblances to their own copyrighted works.

Issue

The core legal issue revolved around intellectual property rights and the originality of AI-generated art. The artists accused CreativAI of copyright infringement, arguing that "Artificial Painter" had unlawfully replicated their unique styles and elements without permission. CreativAI, on the other hand, claimed that the artworks were original creations of their AI, asserting that any similarities were coincidental and a product of the AI's independent "creative process."

Legal proceedings

In this example, a court could have raised unprecedented questions about authorship and originality in the age of AI. The key arguments include the following:

- **Plaintiffs (the artists):** They could have argued that "Artificial Painter" had access to their works and the AI's algorithm essentially 'learned' their styles, leading to derivative works that infringed upon their copyrights.

- **Defendant (CreativAI):** The defense could have centered on the AI's autonomy in creating new works, emphasizing that the AI's process was akin to any human artist being inspired by existing art.

Expert analysis

Legal experts and AI ethicists could have been brought in to dissect the workings of "Artificial Painter." They could have found that while the AI did create novel compositions, its learning process heavily relied on patterns and elements from its training dataset, which included copyrighted materials.

Resolution

A court could have ruled that while AI can assist in the creative process, the output in cases where copyrighted materials are heavily referenced or replicated, even unconsciously, can constitute infringement. The ruling could have acknowledged the complexity of AI creativity but emphasized the need for clear guidelines and ethical boundaries in using copyrighted materials for AI training.

Aftermath and impact

The ruling could have had significant implications, such as the following:

- **AI development**: There was a heightened focus on ethical AI development, with companies investing in creating more transparent algorithms and ensuring diverse, non-infringing datasets.

- **Legal frameworks**: The case could have prompted legal reforms, with discussions on updating copyright laws to better address the realities of AI in creative fields.

- **Art community**: Artists and galleries became more cautious in dealing with AI-generated art, seeking legal advice before exhibitions or sales.

Conclusion

The fictional "Artificial Painter" case study exemplifies the intricate challenges at the intersection of intellectual property rights and generative AI. It highlights the need for a balanced approach that fosters innovation while respecting the rights and creative integrity of human artists. This case serves as a crucial reference point for future AI art endeavors, marking a significant moment in the evolution of art and law in the digital age.

Again, the "Artificial Painter" case study I present is fictional. It is not based on an actual legal case or real events. The intention in creating this fictional case study is to provide a conceptual understanding of the issues that could arise in the evolving area of generative AI.

Summary

In this chapter, we have explored several key themes related to AI and art, focusing specifically on the impact and implications of AI technologies such as DALL-E 3. We emphasized the importance of navigating the ethical and legal landscapes that are evolving with these technological advancements. As we embrace the possibilities brought forth by AI in the art world, we must do so with a mindful approach that respects both the power of technology and the value of human expression.

In the next chapter, we will cover how to craft compelling prompts and get your imagination flowing with customizable prompt templates.

8

Effective Prompt Cheat Sheet

This chapter is a treasure trove of cheat sheets that are designed to transform your journey with DALL-E 3. This chapter is dedicated to turning you into a DALL-E 3 prompt expert, filled to the brim with insightful cheat sheets that make navigating this advanced AI tool a breeze.

We'll focus on how you can be purposeful and precise in your wording to get the most accurate and satisfying outcomes from DALL-E 3. These tips will equip you with the skills to take your AI art creations to the next level. Get ready to transform the way you interact with DALL-E 3, turning your imaginative concepts into stunning visual realities.

Now, let's go through the following topics:

- Crafting compelling prompts
- Cheat sheet
- Sparking imagination through prompts

Crafting compelling prompts

Creating compelling prompts with DALL-E 3 involves a blend of clarity, creativity, and specificity.

In revisiting the ABCs of DALL-E 3 from *Chapter 1*, we are reminded to consider three key elements – artistic style, background, and colors:

- **Artistic style:** This is our first decision. What style should our output be in? It could be anything from realistic to abstract, impressionistic to modern. The style sets the tone for our image. Refer to *Chapter 2* for a recap of the various artistic styles we have explored.

- **Background:** Next, we need to decide on the background. Should it be a simple, uncluttered white, focusing all attention on our subject? Or perhaps a specific setting, such as a beach or a nightclub, would better suit our purpose? The background can dramatically change the context and feel of our image.

- **Colors**: Finally, we have the choice of colors. Do we prefer a monochromatic scheme, maybe black and white with a striking splash of blue for dramatic effect? Or are we aiming for a more vibrant, colorful palette? The colors we choose will significantly influence the mood and impact of our image.

These elements are crucial because, if we don't specify them, DALL-E will make assumptions based on its programming and training. Our choices guide DALL-E in creating an image that aligns with our vision and purpose.

Revisiting prompting tips

Here's how you can craft prompts that effectively communicate your ideas and intentions to the AI, resulting in stunning and relevant visual outputs:

- **Be specific**: Start with clear and detailed descriptions. The more specific your prompt, the more likely DALL-E 3 will generate an image that matches your vision. Include details about the subject, setting, style, and mood you want to convey. For example, instead of saying `a dog`, specify `a golden retriever puppy sitting in a sunlit garden`.

- **Use descriptive language**: Engage with vivid and descriptive language to bring your prompt to life. Words that evoke senses and emotions can add depth and richness to your generated images. For instance, `a tranquil autumn forest with golden leaves gently falling` paints a more vivid picture than `a forest in the fall`.

- **Incorporate artistic styles or themes**: If you have a particular artistic style or theme in mind, include it in your prompt. DALL-E 3 can interpret and replicate various art styles, from impressionism to surrealism, or themes such as futuristic, fantasy, or vintage.

- **Balance detail and creativity**: While specifics are crucial, leave some room for creative interpretation by the AI. This balance can lead to unique and surprising results that might enhance your original concept.

- **Iterate and refine**: Prompt crafting is often an iterative process. Don't hesitate to refine and adjust your prompts based on the outputs you receive. This practice helps in understanding how DALL-E 3 interprets different phrases and terms.

- **Learn from examples**: Look at successful prompts used by others and analyze what makes them effective. This can provide insights and inspiration for your prompts.

Remember, compelling prompts are the key to unlocking the full potential of DALL-E 3. By following these guidelines, you can create prompts that are not only effective in guiding the AI but also in bringing your creative visions to life.

Now, let's dive in and begin exploring our custom cheat sheets!

Cheat sheet

By being precise, we aim to provide enough detail and context to guide the AI toward our desired outcome, while avoiding ambiguity or vagueness that might lead to unexpected or irrelevant results. This involves understanding the capabilities and limitations of the AI system and tailoring our prompts accordingly to achieve the most accurate and effective response. The following cheat sheets will guide you through creating better prompts.

I'll provide you with a customizable prompt to experiment with. Use it as it is but replace the words in the brackets with your own choices. Refer to *Chapter 2* to get ideas on camera angles, positions, creative film types, and more.

Try out this initial prompt for experimentation purposes:

```
Create a [camera angle or position] of a [color, if applicable +
image type] in a [artistic style] with a [background], [lighting
type] or [creative film type]
```

What you'll do now is follow these three simple steps:

1. Copy the prompt.
2. Add your contents within the brackets, [].
3. Run the prompt in DALL-E 3.

I'll create a few examples of my own, using the prompt template, to help get you started. First, we'll create a cherry falling into a glass of water. I want to make it dramatic, and I want to freeze the action of the water splashing, so I'm going to use a fast shutter speed. See *Figure 8.1*.

Prompt: Create a [close-up] of a [red cherry falling into a glass full of water] with a [black background], [low-key lighting], [fast shutter speed]

Figure 8.1: Low-key lighting and fast shutter speed

Now, I want to show an example of a slow shutter speed shot. I'm going to prompt DALL-E 3 to create a nighttime scene of cars driving fast, and this time, we're going to use a slow shutter speed. See *Figure 8.2*.

Prompt: Create a [nighttime] scene of [cars driving fast], [slow shutter speed]

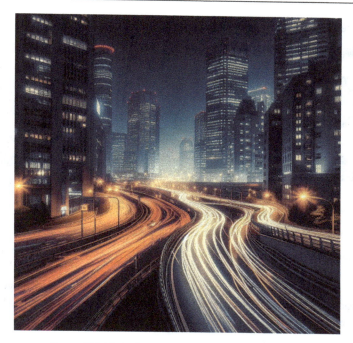

Figure 8.2: Nighttime scene and slow shutter speed

I'll give you a few more fun prompts to get you started on your DALL-E 3 journey but, this time, we'll focus on some practical applications, such as digital ads, product launches, posters, and more.

Facebook ad

Let's say I'm creating a Facebook ad for a fountain pen and want to showcase the product on a high-end piece of furniture to convey the brand's image. See *Figure 8.3*. Let's consider a prompt for this use case.

Prompt: `Create an [image of two fountain pens] for a [Facebook ad] that will [get clicks from people wanting to buy fountain pens], show the [pens on a rich-looking wood desk].`

My example generated two solid images of what I want, so there's no need to iterate!

Figure 8.3: Two fountain pens on a rich wooden desk, created for a Facebook ad to attract potential buyers

Now that we've explored the fascinating capabilities of AI in crafting compelling images for Facebook ads, let's shift our focus to another exciting application of AI in the realm of marketing: creating a product launch poster.

Product launch poster

In this example, I want to create something that will drive sales for my dog collar brand. See *Figure 8.4*.

Prompt: Create a [Dalmatian and an English Bulldog] in a [Whimsical style] for the ["Nub's Collars" product launch poster]

Figure 8.4: Whimsical-style digital artworks for the "Nub's Collars" product
launch poster, featuring a dalmatian and an English bulldog

For a revised prompt, we can ask DALL-E to create an image that focuses more on visual realism and excludes any text elements because I feel this image isn't working well. The revised scene can be described in detail to emphasize its core elements, ensuring clarity and simplicity while maintaining the essence of the original idea. As previously discussed in *Chapter 6*, particularly in *Figure 6.1*, spelling errors are common in AI-generated artwork. This is evident in the incorrect spellings of "Nub's Collars" in *Figure 8.4*.

Iterated prompt: `Create a [Dalmatian] in a [photorealistic style] wearing a [bright red collar] for the ["Nub's Collars" product launch poster]`

Figure 8.5: Photorealistic digital artworks featuring a dalmatian wearing
a bright red collar, created for our dog collar brand

The image in *Figure 8.5* seems a bit too polished for my taste, so I'll refine the prompt – this time, asking for a "natural look" to enhance its realism. Remember, to build upon an image iteratively, you can refine and modify your prompts based on the results of previous image generations. This approach allows you to gradually evolve an image toward your desired outcome. DALL-E's capabilities are bounded by its training and the specificity of the prompts it receives.

Iterated prompt: `Now, with a more natural look.`

Here, DALL-E is getting the hang of my preferences, and I don't need to provide full prompts anymore. If I want a more realistic touch compared to the previous one, I simply tell DALL-E to dial up the realism – that's enough:

Figure 8.6: Natural-looking digital artwork of a dalmatian with a
bright red collar, designed for our dog collar brand

In my last attempt in *Figure 8.6*, the background was overly complex. To simplify it, I requested DALL-E to create a version with a white background, highlighting only the blue eyes and the red collar. This approach resulted in a more impactful and striking image, as shown in *Figure 8.7*:

Figure 8.7: Final image for an ad

It was a four-step journey to perfect our dalmatian image using DALL-E. Just four iterations and we nailed the look we were aiming for – not too bad, if you ask me!

Now, let's dive into the exciting task of crafting an image for a movie poster.

Movie poster

In this section, we'll design a movie poster using a straightforward prompt.

Prompt: `Create a movie poster, [dramatic and cinematic-style], for the upcoming film ["Nine Lives"], featuring [a cat wearing a black mask like Zoro]`

Figure 8.8: Initial image for our movie poster

Our first attempt yielded a design that is quite impressive. As we know, movie posters typically have a rectangular format. Although we have the option to request DALL-E 3 to generate an image in a rectangular shape, such as the `1024px x 1792px` size we explored in *Chapter 3*, we've decided to continue with this square image. We plan to further refine it in a different software. The image showcased in *Figure 8.8* is suitable for our purposes. To complete our poster, we'll import it into a graphic design application, such as Adobe Illustrator. There, we can incorporate textual elements and put the finishing touches on our design. Since our primary focus here is on DALL-E 3 rather than Adobe Illustrator, we will not get into the subsequent steps involving Illustrator.

Next, we'll proceed to develop a YouTube thumbnail. A YouTube thumbnail serves as the small, clickable preview image viewers see when browsing videos on YouTube.

YouTube thumbnail

Let's compose a concise prompt for our YouTube thumbnail. The ideal thumbnail size for YouTube is **1280px × 720px**, adhering to the **16:9 aspect ratio** for best visibility on various screens and devices. You can request an image from DALL-E with dimensions of **1792px x 1024px** to achieve a rectangular shape. Remember, YouTube thumbnails have a size limit of **2 MB**. If the downloaded image from DALL-E exceeds this, you'll need to resize it. One way to do this is by using Adobe Illustrator: open the image, adjust the size to **1280px × 720px**, and change the DPI from **300** to **72**. This process will ensure your image stays under the 2 MB limit and fits the YouTube thumbnail specifications.

Prompt: `Create a [vibrant and eye-catching] YouTube thumbnail featuring a [beach ball], designed to be appealing and suitable for a [wide range of audiences]`

Figure 8.9: YouTube thumbnail

This prompt resulted in a fun and engaging thumbnail, as shown in *Figure 8.9*. So, I'm going to roll with it!

Next up, we'll explore the creative process of prompting to design a logo.

Brand logo

Now, let's dive into our logo design prompt.

Prompt: `Give me two different logo designs for a [pen brand named "Price Pens"]. [Pens] are made of [olive wood]`

Figure 8.10: Logo for a pen brand

As shown in *Figure 8.10*, the prompt yielded impressive results. Had it not met our expectations, we could have iterated on it, much like we did with the Dalmatian in *Figure 8.7*. Note how the word "Price" is misspelled. Keep an eye out for such errors!

Moving on, we will proceed to design a logo for a new cafe.

Prompt: `Create a logo design for a [new cafe called "Espresso Yourself"]`

Figure 8.11: Logo for a cafe

Two images were generated with the prompt; I chose the one that best represented the brand, as shown in *Figure 8.11*.

Now, we'll create a couple of fashion brand logos using different styles.

Prompt: `Create a logo design for a [fashion brand called "Knot Average"]. Use natural colors`

Figure 8.12: Logo for the clothing brand Knot Average

Now, let's modify `Knot Average` by incorporating the word `Your` and specifying `black and gold` colors. This adjustment constitutes a completely new prompt rather than a simple iteration as we are altering several elements. While there's no strict guideline distinguishing a new prompt from an iteration, in this instance, our goal is to generate a distinctly new visual appearance and feel for the logo. See *Figure 8.13*.

Prompt: `Create a logo for a fashion brand called ["Knot Your Average"]. Use [black and gold] as the colors`

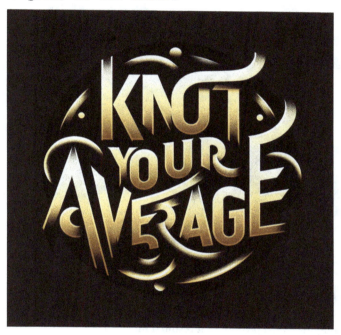

Figure 8.13: Here, we created a new logo for the clothing brand Knot Your Average and changed the colors to black and gold

Now that you know how to create a brand logo, let's move on to designing product packaging.

Product packaging

Let's see a sample product packaging prompt.

Prompt: `Design packaging for a new [tea brand] named ['Izzy's']`

Figure 8.14: Product packaging for a tea brand called Izzy's Tea

Here, we crafted a straightforward prompt that resulted in a visually pleasing design, but it contains a spelling error of an additional "Z" on the top and bottom of the box. In addition, the text on the brochures doesn't match the text on the box; see *Figure 8.14*. We can either iterate to correct the spelling in the design, or we could request a version without text from DALL-E, allowing us to add the correct text later using Adobe Illustrator. I tried three more times, and it finally got the spelling right; see *Figure 8.15*:

Figure 8.15: We iterated product packaging for Izzy's Tea and arrived
at a correctly spelled brand name for the final image

The process of refining the design for the "Izzy's Tea" packaging highlights the dynamic interplay between creativity and precision. By navigating the challenges of design iteration and decision-making, we successfully arrived at a visually appealing and correctly spelled final product.

Having explored the realm of logo design and product packaging, we'll now transition to a different yet equally creative endeavor: crafting a comic strip. This shift takes us from the concise symbolism of logos to the narrative and visual storytelling of comics, where characters and plots come to life through sequential art. Let's dive into this new, imaginative process.

Comic strip

Let's look at an example to see how we can craft a prompt for a comic strip.

Prompt: `Create a [four-panel] comic strip set on the [beach]. [Panel 1: Mochi, a cute, fluffy dog, is playfully exploring the beach on his skateboard. Panel 2: A dog fairy, resembling Mochi with wings and a little wand, appears, surprising Mochi. Both dogs look almost identical. Panel 3: A cute bunny hops into the scene, looking friendly and playful. Panel 4: All characters, are playing happily at the beach under the blue sky]`

Figure 8.16: Four-panel comic strip

In reviewing the comic strip, it's evident that some aspects were executed as intended, while others deviated from our request. We successfully received a four-panel comic strip as requested. Our original vision included three characters: a dog, a dog fairy, and a bunny. However, the outcome differed slightly, featuring two characters – a dog and a bunny fairy, instead of the three specified.

Next, let's tackle something a bit more intricate: a life cycle diagram.

Life cycle diagram

This prompt presents a more complex and nuanced challenge compared to our usual ones. Creating a life cycle diagram will likely require multiple attempts. In my experience, OpenAI's platform tends to require fewer iterations for such tasks than Bing. Therefore, I recommend using OpenAI to generate a life cycle diagram. One issue I often encounter with Bing in producing life cycle diagrams is aligning all the arrows correctly (if the diagram includes arrows). It's also a bit tricky to arrange our subjects in the correct sequence without explicit instructions on placement. To illustrate this, I'll use the simplest concept I can think of: a diagram showing the progression from a seed to a blooming flower.

I will demonstrate the same prompt on both Bing and OpenAI to provide you with a clearer comparison of the output each generates using the identical prompt.

After seven attempts on Bing, with my seventh prompt shown in *Figure 8.17*, I decided to switch to OpenAI to achieve a result more aligned with what I had in mind.

Prompt: Create a [diagram that will explain the life cycle of a flower].
Show four sections, first a seed, second a seed getting water and
starting to grow, third a seed getting sun and starting to grow
more, and fourth a fully grown flower

Figure 8.17: Life cycle created with DALL-E 3 using Bing Image Creator

As we can see, Bing didn't accurately interpret my requests to create images with arrows pointing in the same direction – the results appear somewhat chaotic. Hence, I decided to attempt this using OpenAI.

We'll use the same prompt, but this time with OpenAI:

 You

create a diagram that will explain the lifecycle of a flower. Show four sections, first a seed, second a seed getting water and starting to grow, third a seed getting sun and starting to grow more, and fourth a fully grown flower

 DALL·E

Figure 8.18: Life cycle created with DALL-E 3 using OpenAI

From these diagrams, you'll see neither is perfectly what I was looking for, but with OpenAI in *Figure 8.18*, we got a lot closer, so I kept iterating with OpenAI.

Now, because I noticed that DALL-E was still a little bit confused, I made the prompt simpler to follow by using a follow-up prompt.

Iterated prompt: `Try again with only three sections: seed, bud, bloom`

Figure 8.19: Seed, bud, and bloom iterated prompt

In *Figure 8.19*, you'll notice I achieved a result closer to my goal by refining my prompt to be more concise. This example shows how it can sometimes be challenging to iterate until you get the image you want. This should aid you in navigating similar iterative challenges in your projects.

Now that you've got the hang of this, let's proceed to create some engaging images to accompany blog posts.

Visuals for a blog post or article

Now, we'll compose a prompt for generating a visual to accompany a magazine article.

Prompt: `[Cartoon-style] images of a [mischievous-looking dog sitting and giving its paw]`

Figure 8.20: Creating a cartoon-style dog for an article

Here, we've created an image featuring an adorable, cartoon-style dog with a mischievous look, sitting and offering its paw.

Example 1

For a blog post titled *Choosing the Right Dog Breed for You*, we could consider featuring various images of different dogs, beginning with a prompt such as the following; see *Figure 8.21*.

Prompt: `Create a [photorealistic] [Pug puppy, English Bulldog puppy, and Chow puppy,] [playing in a park], [golden hour]`

Figure 8.21: Three puppies for example 1

I feel like the initial image didn't sufficiently capture the essence of my blog post, so I opted for a more descriptive approach, focusing on the dogs' personalities. This led me to craft a more detailed prompt.

Iterated prompt: `Try again, but have each dog do something reminiscent of their personalities based on their breed type`

Figure 8.22: Final image for example 1

Figure 8.22 isn't exactly what I had in mind either, but you know what? It's so different and cool in its own way that I'm just going to roll with it!

Example 2

Next up, we're going to create an image for a blog post about picking the perfect lip gloss. I'm thinking of an image with a bunch of different lip gloss colors, and I want it to be really fun. I'm going to keep the prompt super simple this time and skip adding a background. I want a close-up shot that's all about the lips, really highlighting them. Here's the prompt I'm going with.

Prompt: `[Close-up]` of `[lips showing different colored lip gloss samples]`

Figure 8.23: Final image for example 2, close-up of lips showing different colored lip gloss samples

I'm satisfied with the first image we made in *Figure 8.23*, so there's no need to make any changes.

Next, we'll explore some additional prompt templates that might be beneficial for you as a designer.

Fashion design

Let's begin with a basic prompt and then expand upon it.

Prompt: `Design a [cocktail dress] for a fashion show.`

Now, we were quite broad in our description, so DALL-E will make certain assumptions. However, we can begin with these assumptions and refine our approach through iteration:

Figure 8.24: Here, we created a cocktail dress for a fashion show

I'm not too fond of this futuristic design, so I'll ask DALL-E to incorporate a different texture and color. Let's include more precise details.

Iterated prompt: Now, make the dress a short black dress with an asymmetrical design made of ostrich feathers

Figure 8.25: Here, we iterated a cocktail dress with an asymmetrical design made of ostrich feathers

If the design I've created isn't quite right, I have the option to continue tweaking various elements, such as color, style, fabric, and more, until the desired result is achieved, similar to the process I employed to arrive at *Figure 8.25*.

I'm quite fond of the design, yet there's room for more creativity. We could explore beyond the conventional and craft something unique using ordinary, unassuming objects. In a creative twist, imagine a fashion line inspired by the eclectic and diverse elements found on the streets of New York. This concept echoes the whimsical idea portrayed in the fictional world of Zoolander, where a unique fashion line, named Derelicte, showcases designs using everyday street items. It's a nod to innovative fashion that pushes boundaries, much like John Galliano's real fashion line from 2000, which creatively incorporated ordinary objects into high fashion.

Let's craft a new prompt while keeping that innovative and creative spirit at the forefront.

Prompt: `Clothing made from everyday objects that could be found on the streets of New York`

Figure 8.26: Iterate clothing design with unassuming objects

From the result, it's evident that the concept of utilizing everyday items to create a dress was executed in a fun and imaginative way.

Now, let's dive into the realm of architectural design and have some creative fun with it!

Architectural design

Let's request DALL-E's assistance in creating an architectural design.

Prompt: `Create an architectural design of a [Mediterranean house]`

Figure 8.27: Creating an architectural design

The result is exactly what we asked for. If we want to have a little more fun with our imagination, we can ask for anything our mind can think of and see what it produces, as depicted when using the following prompt to create the image shown in *Figure 8.28*.

Prompt: `Create an architectural design of a house inspired by the Vegas strip`

Figure 8.28: House inspired by the Vegas strip

Now that we've had some fun with house designs, let's move on to 3D renderings.

3D model

A 3D isometric illustration presents a scene or object in a way that shows three-dimensional depth and structure but without the perspective distortion seen in typical 3D representations. It provides a clear, detailed view of all sides of the object, often used in technical and architectural visualizations because it can accurately depict measurements and spatial relationships in a visually appealing way.

Prompt: `Create a 3D isometric model of an [upscale horse barn]`

Figure 8.29: 3D isometric illustration

The prompt resulted in a beautiful 3D illustration of an upscale horse barn, highlighting elements of luxury and sophistication in its design.

> **Important note**
>
> Previously, using this prompt didn't lead to any complications, but recently, it has become sensitive to terms such as "3D model." To navigate this, you might need to experiment with different phrasings to achieve the desired result. For instance, I found that replacing "3D model" with "3D isometric illustration" was more effective in getting the outcome I wanted.

Mock magazine cover

We're creating this magazine cover not as a final product but rather as part of a creative brainstorming session. This approach allows us to visualize our ideas in a cover format, making it an effective way to present them to our boss or the decision-maker for our magazine cover – and that person might even be you! After choosing a design we like, the next step would be to execute the actual cover, although that's not something we'll be doing here. Refer to *Chapter 6* for information on standard sizes used in magazine covers.

Prompt: `Design a magazine cover for a [travel magazine called "Culinary Journeys Around the World"]`

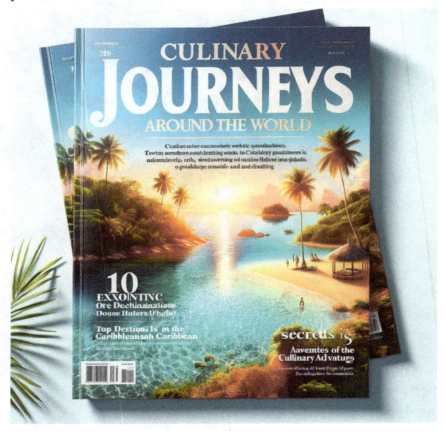

Figure 8.30: Mock magazine cover

The mockup shown in *Figure 8.30* ended up being the ideal representation for presenting our concept for the **Culinary Journeys Around the World** magazine cover. If this one didn't meet our expectations, we would have continued iterating until we found a design that truly matched our vision.

Now, let's learn how to create children's book illustrations.

Children's book illustration

To write a prompt for a children's book illustration, we'll focus on crafting a vivid and imaginative description that captures the essence of the scene or character we want to depict. We'll include key details, such as the setting, the main characters, and any important objects or themes, ensuring we infuse the description with elements that are appealing and appropriate for a young audience. Refer to *Chapter 6* for more information on standard sizes used in book covers.

Prompt: `Create an illustration for a children's book featuring [a cute lobster exploring a colorful underwater land]`

Figure 8.31: Children's book illustration

This clear and well-crafted prompt yielded exactly the results we were looking for. Next, let's proceed to create an illustration that's suitable for a coloring book.

Coloring book

When creating a prompt for a coloring book illustration, our goal is to describe a scene or character that's both engaging and suitable for coloring. We'll focus on outlining clear, simple elements that can be easily translated into line art.

Prompt: `Design a coloring book page featuring ['Nub', the Shitzu-Pomeranian mix dog, and his Maine Coon cat friend, 'Salty']`

This prompt is intriguing because, although I included the names of the pets in it, these names are not visible in the illustration. To have names appear in an image, they must be explicitly specified in the prompt, unless you are creating a logo or similar content where text is automatically generated:

Figure 8.32: Coloring book illustration

With that, we've finished designing an illustration for a coloring book. Next, we'll spark your imagination through some out-of-the-box thinking to ignite your creativity and expand your horizons.

Sparking imagination through prompts

To jumpstart your creativity, we're going to dive into a series of zany and entertaining ideas to set your imagination in motion. Let's begin by generating some images that reflect your style and preferences, as I've done in *Figure 8.33*.

Creating your own character

Let's look at this prompt to create my own character:

Prompt: `Create a 3D illustration of an animated character sitting casually on top of a social media logo "Facebook". The character is a 40-year-old woman, with brown eyes with winged eyeliner, long shiny dark brown hair, wearing a black beret hat, a black scoop neck tank top, and pants with black shoes. The background of the image is a social media profile page with the username "holly_picano".`

Figure 8.33: 3D illustration of an animated character with the Facebook logo

I'm pleased with the character design; it's charming and aligns closely with our request. Although it's unclear whether she's sitting atop the social media logo and we can't see the color of her shoes, that's fine. Next, we plan to explore a similar concept for a LinkedIn profile:

Prompt: `Create a 3D illustration of an animated character sitting casually on top of a social media logo "LinkedIn". The character is a [40-year-old woman, with brown eyes, and long shiny brown hair, wearing a black beret hat, black turtleneck shirt, and pants with black shoes]. The background of the image is a social media profile page with a username of ["holly-picano-481a872"] and a profile picture that matches the animated character.`

Figure 8.34: 3D illustration of an animated character with the LinkedIn logo

You can experiment with designing your own profile picture by using various poses and incorporating social media icons. In the prompt, I mentioned my entire LinkedIn profile name, `holly-picano-481a872` but one of the numbers is missing in my image. I'm okay with this because I know people will find me if they search my name.

Similar to *Figure 8.34*, where we created a profile picture, we're going to create a similar design using a cell phone with the following prompt. See *Figure 8.35*.

Prompt: `American-Italian lady with glasses, wears a black t-shirt written "Holly", denim jacket, black jeans, as if she wants to get out of the broken iPhone 13 screen, one leg is out, both hands are holding on the side of the screen, various icons of Facebook, WhatsApp, Instagram, etc. , and colorful water splashes spreading in the background create realistic 3D and high-resolution HD work. Black background.`

Figure 8.35: Profile on cell phone

I'm interested in exploring a new concept and I'm confident that DALL-E 3 will incorporate my brown hair and eyes into the image if I request an illustration of "Holly," given my history of creating my own character. Next, I plan to request an illustration of Holly as a superhero. There's no need to specify my brown hair and eyes again as this has already been established. Consequently, I'll consider this request as an iterative prompt, despite the distinct changes in background and costume I'm seeking compared to previous requests.

Iterated prompt: Now, a 3D illustrations of Holly as a superhero dressed in colors of blue and red, busting out of a wall, without any specific logo in the background, focusing on her heroism amidst a generic urban setting.

Figure 8.36: Iterated image of Holly as a superhero

Now that we've enjoyed making animated profile pictures, let's try designing a house in a unique and unconventional setting. By experimenting like this, you'll start to grasp the potential of DALL-E and discover new ways to create things beyond your wildest imagination.

Creating out-of-the-ordinary settings

Consider this prompt:

Prompt: `Create an architectural design of a house completely underwater`

Figure 8.37: Underwater house

This concept of an underwater house can inspire innovative ideas in futuristic living and challenge conventional design norms. Additionally, for content creators who specialize in showcasing distinctive homes, interior design, or environmental themes, this concept offers a visually captivating feature to attract and engage their audience.

Now, let's try out a concept where a woman is adorned in a dress made of water, as shown in *Figure 8.38*.

Prompt: `Woman wearing a dress made of water`

Figure 8.38: Woman wearing a water dress

You'll discover that even from the simplest prompt, we can craft an incredibly imaginative and creative piece. Next, we'll craft a more intricate prompt to generate another image of something extraordinary and beyond the realm of reality, demonstrating the capabilities of DALL-E.

Prompt: `Create an imaginative and colorful image of butterflies flying underwater. These butterflies should be depicted in various sizes and vibrant colors, fluttering their wings gracefully as if swimming through the water. The underwater environment should be a vivid and lively scene, filled with coral reefs, schools of fish, and aquatic plants`

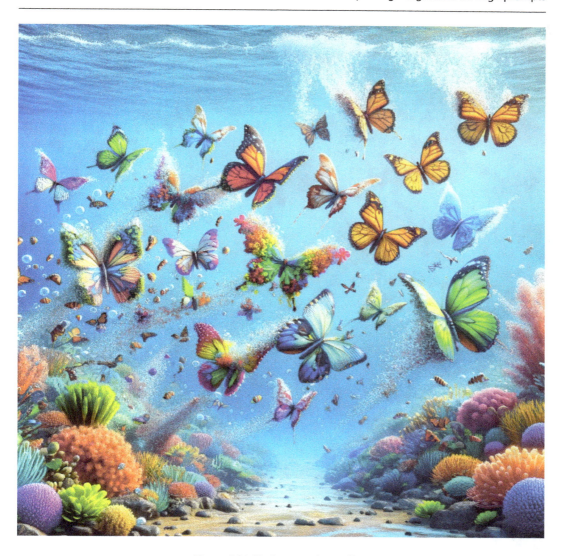

Figure 8.39: Underwater butterflies

As demonstrated in *Figure 8.39*, by creating an image of butterflies flying underwater, something that defies natural occurrences, we can see that DALL-E enables us to bring even the most imaginative concepts to visual life. If we can envision it, DALL-E can depict it.

To conclude this section on a high note, I'll present one final image. Let's envision and create a scene in which `dolphins soar gracefully above the clouds`:

Figure 8.40: Flying dolphins

As we consider the example of dolphins flying in the sky in *Figure 8.40*, we're reminded of the power of stepping outside conventional thinking. This imaginative scenario inspires us to break free from the usual constraints of logic and reality. In visualizing such an extraordinary scene, we encourage ourselves to embrace creative thinking, diving into ideas and concepts that defy what's typical. It's a liberating exercise in creative exploration, reminding us that in the realm of imagination, there are no limits.

Let's wrap up this chapter by engaging in an entertaining quiz to explore some of the well-known limitations of DALL-E 3.

Limitation exploration quiz

Here are some figures that showcase known limitations of DALL-E (such as handling text within images or generating specific, intricate details accurately).

Look at the images in the following subsections and determine which are inaccurate.

Text in images

We have discussed that DALL-E can struggle with accurately placing coherent and contextually correct text within images. For example, generating a book cover with specific title text and author names often results in jumbled or nonsensical characters.

Let's consider this prompt: `Create a mockup book cover with the title "It's a Sultry Night in London". The book should be in natural colors, it's on a desk in a moody dark office.`

We've already covered the fact that DALL-E 3 usually gets text right about 50% of the time. Here, you'll notice that very point. Which one is inaccurate?

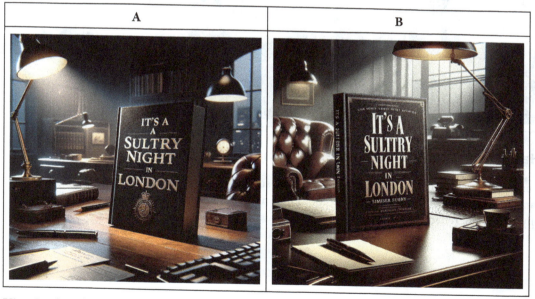

Hint: Look at the spelling of "Sultry."

Consistent multi-image narratives

Generating a series of images that tell a consistent and coherent story can be difficult for DALL-E. While individual images may be high-quality, maintaining narrative consistency across multiple generated images is challenging.

Let's consider this prompt: `A cute ladybug that is taking a journey from walking upon the soil in a garden to eventually making it onto a flower, which was his goal.`

Here, you will notice that one of the multi-image narratives doesn't bring our character to its goal. Which one is inaccurate?

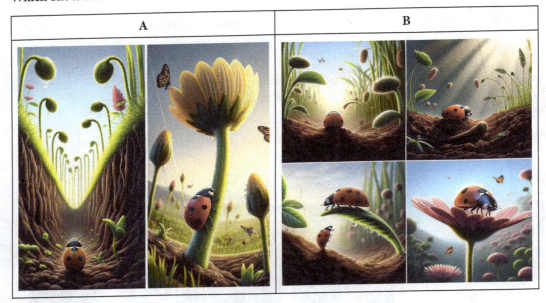

Handling reflective surfaces and materials

Generating images that accurately depict reflective surfaces, such as mirrors, water, or shiny metals, can be a challenge for DALL-E. The reflections may not accurately represent the surroundings or the physics of light reflection.

For instance, take this prompt: `Create an image of a girl reaching out to touch a mirror with her right hand. You see her reflection in the mirror.`

In this example, you can see the lady's reflection. Which one is inaccurate?

A	B

Within image **B**, the lady's face would probably need to be a lot closer to the mirror to see the reflection from our angle, but other than that, it looks pretty accurate! In image **A**, the lady's hand is coming right out of the mirror, as you can see her fingers (on the mirror side) extend slightly further than the frame on the mirror. In addition, she's extending her left hand, not her right hand.

Let's give the mirror images another try. This time, we'll include a fluffy cat. Let's consider this prompt:

`Fluffy Persian cat with both paws placed on a mirror, capturing a moment of curiosity and wonder. Set in an elegantly furnished room, each image portrays the cat's playful yet majestic nature, emphasizing its luxurious coat and the enchanting moment of self-discovery.`

In this example, you can see the cat's reflection. Which one is inaccurate?

A	B

One of the photos is nearly perfect, while the other captures a paw extending beyond the frame as if it's playfully interacting with the mirror. It feels like a serendipitous moment, creating a surprisingly captivating effect!

We hope you've enjoyed exploring DALL-E 3's limitations through these illustrative examples.

Summary

In this chapter, we explored the art and skill of creating compelling prompts, mastering precision in purposeful prompting, and sparking imagination through prompts. Each of these elements plays a crucial role in effectively harnessing the potential of AI such as DALL-E. By crafting compelling prompts, we learned to communicate our ideas clearly and creatively, ensuring that the AI accurately reflects our vision. Precision in prompting taught us the importance of detail and specificity, enabling us to fine-tune our requests for more tailored results. And through sparking imagination with prompts, we explored the boundless realms of creativity, stretching our minds to conceive the unconventional and the extraordinary.

As we move on to the final chapter of this book, we'll transition from the theoretical and practical aspects of AI interaction to the real world. We'll dive into interviews with experts in AI and examine case studies, providing a comprehensive view of how these skills are applied in various fields. This is the natural next step – that is, building on our foundational knowledge and understanding, and seeing it come to life in diverse, real-world scenarios.

9

Case Studies, Interviews, and Insights

In this chapter, we look into the practical applications and transformative potential of DALL-E 3 through a series of detailed case studies and insightful interviews. While the chapter title hints at our focus, it's important to articulate not just what we will explore but why these explorations are crucial.

Interviews with pioneers and experts in the field further enrich our exploration. These conversations offer deep insights into the evolving landscape of generative AI, revealing the thought processes, ethical considerations, and future aspirations of those at the forefront of this technology. By engaging directly with these voices, we gain a multifaceted perspective on what it means to work with AI software such as DALL-E 3.

The purpose of this chapter is not only to inform but also to inspire. By examining specific instances of DALL-E 3's application and listening to the experts' visions, you will gain a comprehensive understanding of generative AI's capabilities, and its potential to reshape our world.

By the end of this chapter, you will be equipped with a deeper understanding of how AI is transforming industries and societies. You will have developed the skills to critically analyze AI case studies, understand the perspectives of AI professionals, and apply this knowledge to real-world scenarios.

We're going to cover the following areas:

- Use cases
- Case studies
- Interviews with experts

Use cases

Let's get into a real-world scenario where DALL-E 3 is making a significant impact. These use cases will not only demonstrate the broad spectrum of DALL-E 3's applications in different fields but will also highlight both the challenges and successes faced by organizations and individuals when incorporating this innovative AI solution. From creative arts to marketing and from educational content to interior design, we will explore how DALL-E 3 is being harnessed to transform and enhance visual creativity and productivity, offering insights into its practical use and the experiences gained during its deployment.

Here are five use cases for DALL-E 3:

- **Creative art and design**: Artists and designers can use DALL-E 3 to generate unique and imaginative artwork or design elements, as we saw in *Chapter 4*, where we learned about using DALL-E 3 to craft fine art prints. Additionally, see *Figure 9.1* for an example of a design we created for an art exhibit:

Figure 9.1: Artwork generated to print out on canvas and hang for an art gallery exhibit

- **Advertising and marketing**: Marketing professionals can utilize DALL-E 3 to generate visually appealing and attention-grabbing images for advertising campaigns, social media content, and promotional materials. It can create custom illustrations, product mockups, or scenarios that might be difficult or expensive to produce with traditional photography. See *Figure 9.2*, which we also created back in *Chapter 8*, as an example of a product mockup:

Figure 9.2: Product mockup of Izzy's Tea

- **Educational content and illustrations**: In the education sector, DALL-E 3 can be used to create diagrams and illustrations for textbooks, educational websites, or online courses. It can generate images that explain complex concepts, historical events, scientific phenomena, or abstract ideas, making learning more engaging and visual. See *Figure 9.3*, which is an example from *Chapter 8*:

Figure 9.3: Educational illustration of a flower from seed to bloom

- **Film and game concept art**: In the entertainment industry, DALL-E 3 can assist in generating concept art for films, video games, or animations. This can include character designs, environment art, or visual ideas for scenes and settings. It can significantly speed up the brainstorming and conceptualization process in creative projects (see *Figure 9.4*):

Figure 9.4: Concept for a video game character

- **Interior design and architecture**: DALL-E 3 can be employed to visualize interior design ideas, architectural concepts, or urban planning projects. It can generate images of furnished rooms, buildings, or cityscapes based on specific descriptions or requirements, providing a visual aid for designers, architects, and their clients (see *Figure 9.5*):

Figure 9.5: Interior design concept

We can see that DALL-E 3 holds transformative potential for a variety of industries, particularly those where visual innovation and design play a critical role. **Real estate**, with its need for compelling property presentations, is another field that can greatly benefit from the virtual staging capabilities offered by DALL-E 3. This technology can enable agents to furnish and decorate properties virtually, showcasing multiple aesthetic options to potential buyers without the physical and financial constraints of traditional staging. In the **fashion industry**, designers and brands can use DALL-E 3 to revolutionize the way they conceptualize and visualize new collections. By generating unique patterns, textures, and designs, DALL-E 3 can dramatically reduce the time and cost associated with developing new fashion lines, from haute couture to everyday wear. The **event planning** sector stands to gain immensely from DALL-E 3's ability, too, by using it to create detailed and realistic visual proposals. Planners can present clients with vivid representations of event themes, decorations, and layouts, facilitating a more collaborative and imaginative planning process.

Now that we have explored the various applications and potential of DALL-E 3 in different industries, let's examine its use in detail with case studies.

Case studies

In this section, we'll go deeper into detailed case studies from the various industries highlighted in our earlier discussion on use cases to illuminate the extensive range of applications for DALL-E 3. While we've previously outlined how this technology can innovate within creative arts, marketing, educational content, and interior design, our case studies aim to further bridge the gap between theoretical application and practical utility. By examining real-world examples of DALL-E 3 in action, we seek not only to underscore the versatility and transformative potential of this tool but also to share tangible insights and lessons learned from its deployment across these sectors.

We now venture into specific case studies that showcase the technology's real-world impact across diverse sectors. These sectors represent a fraction of the vast possibilities for DALL-E 3's integration, highlighting its practical utility and the transformative potential it holds for businesses looking to innovate and enhance their visual creativity and productivity.

Case 1 – Digital artist – Creating an exhibition with DALL-E 3

Utilizing DALL-E 3 to create art for an exhibition opens up innovative pathways for curators and artists alike, blending cutting-edge AI technology with the timeless pursuit of artistic expression. The resulting art can engage audiences in unique ways, sparking conversations and reflections on the role of AI in creative processes and the future of art itself, making exhibitions not just a showcase of talent but a forum for dialog on innovation and creativity.

This case study focuses on a digital artist, Emma, who specializes in graphic design and multimedia art.

Objective

Emma aimed to create a unique series of digital artworks for an upcoming exhibition, which required innovative and surreal imagery. Her goal was to blend traditional artistic elements with futuristic concepts, which was a challenge given her limited time and resources.

Implementation

Let's dive into the specific steps Emma took to realize her artistic objective, showcasing the potential of AI as a tool for artistic innovation and expression.

1. **Initial exploration**: Emma started by inputting basic concepts into DALL-E 3, using descriptive phrases that encapsulated her vision, such as `"futuristic cityscape with surreal elements"` or `"abstract representation of time in a digital world."`
2. **Refinement**: Based on initial outputs, she refined her prompts, incorporating more specific descriptions and styles, such as `"a cityscape in the style of Salvador Dalí"` (see *Figure 9.6*) or `"abstract clocks melting in a digital landscape."`

3. **Integration and iteration**: Emma used the generated images as foundational elements. She further processed these images using her skills in digital editing, integrating them into larger compositions, and iterating based on aesthetic judgment and thematic consistency. Refer to *Chapter 6* to learn how to change the output size and add text to the final image.

4. **Collaboration and feedback**: Emma shared these images with her peers for feedback, further tweaking them based on suggestions and even using DALL-E 3 to generate variations based on this feedback.

Results

Let's explore the outcomes of Emma's project utilizing DALL-E 3:

- **Enhanced creativity**: DALL-E 3 enabled Emma to explore creative avenues that she hadn't considered, pushing the boundaries of her artistic expression

- **Time efficiency**: The tool significantly reduced the time required for conceptualization and initial creation, allowing Emma to focus on refinement and execution

- **Unique artworks**: The final series was a collection of visually striking and thematically coherent artworks that received acclaim for their originality and imaginative depth:

Figure 9.6: Futuristic cityscape with surreal elements in the style of Salvador Dalí

Conclusion

DALL-E 3 served not just as a tool for image generation but as a collaborative partner in the creative process for Emma. By integrating DALL-E 3's outputs with digital editing and valuing peer feedback, she not only achieved thematic consistency and aesthetic depth in her compositions but also demonstrated the iterative and collaborative nature of modern digital art creation.

Having explored Emma's innovative journey with DALL-E 3 in the realm of art, we will now turn our attention to how DALL-E 3 can revolutionize the field of marketing.

Case 2 – The advertising revolution using DALL-E 3

In this case study, we examine a mid-sized marketing firm, **InnovateX**, that specializes in digital marketing and has a diverse clientele ranging from tech startups to lifestyle brands.

Objective

InnovateX is driven by the desire to enhance the visual appeal and creativity of their campaigns and social media content. Their goal is to craft unique, eye-catching visuals that not only captivate but also stand out in the highly competitive digital arena, achieving this through the cost-effective and efficient production of custom illustrations and product mockups.

Implementation

In this segment, we will track InnovateX's process as they craft social media content, design illustrations, and develop tailored mockups for their clientele:

1. **Initial trials**: InnovateX began by using DALL-E 3 to generate images for a social media campaign for a tech start-up. The prompts included futuristic technology in everyday settings, aiming to illustrate the accessibility and innovation of the client's product.

2. **Expanding the scope**: Encouraged by the initial success, the firm started utilizing DALL-E 3 for a wider range of clients. For a fashion brand, they generated custom illustrations showcasing clothing in abstract artistic settings (see *Figure 9.7*):

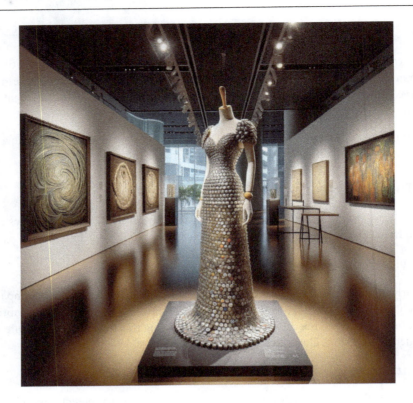

Figure 9.7: Fashion illustration showcasing clothing in an artistic setting

3. **Custom product mockups**: For clients with physical products, DALL-E 3 was used to create product mockups in various scenarios. This was particularly useful for conceptual products or for visualizing products in environments that would be logistically challenging to arrange in real life (see *Figure 9.8*):

Figure 9.8: Product mockup of a gym shoe in an environment
that would be challenging to arrange in real life

4. **Campaign integration and feedback**: The generated images were integrated into various digital campaigns and shared on social media platforms. The firm closely monitored engagement metrics and gathered audience feedback to refine its approach.

Results

Let's explore the outcomes of InnovateX's project utilizing DALL-E 3:

- **Cost and time efficiency**: The use of AI-generated images reduced the reliance on traditional photography and graphic design, leading to lower production costs and faster turnaround times

- **Increased engagement**: The campaigns incorporating DALL-E 3 images showed a significant increase in engagement rates, including likes, shares, and comments

- **Creative expansion**: DALL-E 3 allowed for greater creative exploration, enabling the creation of visuals that were previously considered too challenging or expensive to produce

Conclusion

DALL-E 3 became an invaluable asset for InnovateX, enhancing their marketing and advertising capabilities. It enabled the firm to produce high-quality, creative visuals at a fraction of the usual cost and time, leading to more dynamic and successful advertising campaigns.

This case study showcases how DALL-E 3 exemplifies the transformative potential of AI in advertising strategies, offering innovative and cost-effective solutions to the traditional challenges faced in marketing and visual content creation. Let's look at a case study highlighting DALL-E 3's role in the education sector.

Case 3 – Revolutionizing educational content with DALL-E 3

This case study focuses on **Quantum Minds Press**, a company specializing in developing educational materials.

Objective

Quantum Minds Press aims to enhance the visual quality and effectiveness of their educational illustrations within their science textbooks. The goal was to make concepts more understandable and engaging through vivid illustrations.

Implementation

In this section, we will track Quantum Minds Press's process as they craft science illustrations for one of their textbooks:

1. **Concept visualization**: Initially, Quantum Mind Press used DALL-E 3 to generate images for complex scientific concepts. For example, they created illustrations explaining the workings of a volcano.

2. **Interactive learning materials**: They generated custom illustrations that could be used in interactive quizzes and educational games.

3. **Textbook illustration**: For textbook production, DALL-E 3 was employed to create diagrams and scenes that complemented the educational content. This included visuals for science textbooks, showing illustrations of the volcanos.

4. **Feedback and refinement**: Upon integrating these images into their materials, EdTech gathered feedback from educators and students. This feedback was used to refine the prompts and improve the relevance and accuracy of the illustrations:

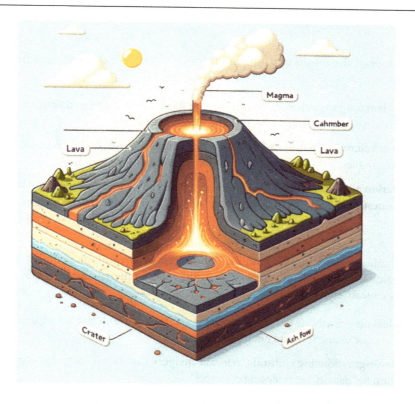

Figure 9.9: Textbook illustration of a volcano

> **Important note**
>
> Keep in mind that verifying the correctness of the generated images falls under your responsibility. For instance, in *Figure 9.9*, one of the labels is incorrectly titled "Cahmber," which is a misspelling. Furthermore, the label "Crater" inaccurately points to a location that is not an actual crater. In this case, we'd iterate until we receive an acceptable outcome or use a tool, such as Canva or Adobe Illustrator, to complete the project, as we learned in *Chapter 6*.

Results

Now let's take a look at the results encountered from Quantum Mind Press's implementation of DALL-E 3:

- **Enhanced learning experience**: The visual aids significantly improved student engagement and comprehension, particularly in complex subject areas.

- **Resource efficiency**: The use of DALL-E 3 expedited the process of creating educational illustrations, reducing the time and cost compared to traditional methods.

- **Customization and scalability**: DALL-E 3 allowed for the easy customization of images to suit different educational contexts and age groups, offering a scalable solution for content creation.

Conclusion

DALL-E 3 has significantly impacted Quantum Mind Press by streamlining content creation and enhancing educational material quality, making learning more immersive and engaging. DALL-E 3 can revolutionize education via the following:

- **Gamified learning**: Enabling the creation of dynamic, interactive elements for gamified learning, including unique characters and environments

- **Visual learning**: Producing culturally relevant imagery that aids in language comprehension and retention by visually representing concepts

- **Aid for disabled learners**: Creating tailored visual content for learners with disabilities, such as simplified illustrations for cognitive disabilities and high-contrast images for the visually impaired

These advancements will provide personalized and accessible learning experiences at reduced costs. Let's look at another application of DALL-E 3 through a case study of video games.

Case 4 – DALL-E 3 enhances the concept art for science fiction video games

This case study examines the role of DALL-E 3 in the development of concept art for "Orion's Quest," which is a high-profile science fiction video game developed by the renowned gaming studio Nova Interactive. The project required extensive and diverse concept art, including character designs, environment art, and scene settings.

Objective

The goal for Nova Interactive was to craft distinctive concept art for scenes, characters, and storyline elements, which are essential in defining a unique visual style for Orion's Quest. This approach was designed to carve out a notable presence for the game in the crowded sci-fi gaming market by focusing on creating engaging and visually striking environments, compelling characters with depth, and a narrative that resonates with players.

Implementation

In this segment, we'll look at Nova Interactive's creative design process for their latest game, Orion's Quest:

1. **Initial concept generation**: The design team used DALL-E 3 to generate initial concepts. They input descriptions such as "`futuristic alien cityscape`" or "`cybernetic space warrior`" to get a wide range of visual ideas.

2. **Design refinement**: The most promising images were selected and further refined. The team used DALL-E 3 to iterate on these concepts, adjusting details to fit the game's narrative and aesthetic requirements.

3. **Integration and feedback loop**: The concept art was presented to the project's creative director and team for feedback. Based on this, further iterations were made using DALL-E 3 to fine-tune the designs.

Results

The outcomes of Nova Interactive's innovative approach to designing Orion's Quest were remarkable, showcasing significant improvements in time and resource efficiency, the development of a unique visual style, and an enhanced creative process in the following aspects:

- **Time and resource efficiency**: The conceptual phase of the project was completed much faster than traditional methods, allowing more time for development and refinement

- **Unique and cohesive art style**: The final concept art for Orion's Quest was acclaimed for its originality and coherence, contributing to the game's distinctive visual identity

- **Enhanced creative process**: DALL-E 3 significantly broadened the creative possibilities, providing the team with a vast array of initial ideas to work from

Conclusion

DALL-E 3 enabled the creation of complex scenes, intricate character designs, and richly detailed storyboards for Orion's Quest. It enhanced the development process by supporting rapid prototyping and iteration with unprecedented speed and efficiency.

In the following section, we will look into how DALL-E 3 is revolutionizing interior design and architecture by offering unprecedented tools for visualization and design that promise to redefine the way spaces are conceived and executed.

Case 5 – Transforming interior design and architecture with DALL-E 3

This case study explores the application of DALL-E 3 by **The Outlier Group**, an innovative interior design and architectural firm. The Outlier Group utilized DALL-E 3 to visualize and present interior design concepts, architectural structures, and urban planning ideas to their clients.

Objective

The Outlier Group aimed to enhance their design process by incorporating DALL-E 3 for the rapid and detailed visualization of their concepts. The goal was to provide clients with vivid, accurate representations of design ideas, facilitating better communication and decision-making.

Implementation

Let's explore the measures The Outlier Group adopted to integrate DALL-E 3 into their strategic framework:

1. **Urban planning scenarios**: In urban planning projects, the tool was used to create detailed cityscapes showing proposed developments, green spaces, and transportation networks.

Figure 9.10: Sustainable urban apartment building

2. **Architectural concept development**: For architectural projects, DALL-E 3 was employed to visualize building exteriors and structures. The Outlier Group input descriptions such as "`sustainable urban apartment building`" or "`futuristic commercial complex`" to generate concepts (see *Figure 9.10*):

3. **Interior design visualization**: The firm used DALL-E 3 to generate images of furnished rooms based on specific themes and requirements. For example, creating a modern minimalist living room or a rustic kitchen (see *Figure 9.11*):

Figure 9.11: Creation of a rustic kitchen

4. **Client presentations and feedback**: These visualizations were presented to clients who could better understand and engage with the proposed ideas. Feedback from the clients was used for further iterations and refinements.

Results

Now let's review the outcomes of The Outlier Group's application of DALL-E 3 in their architectural and interior design endeavors:

- **Streamlined design process**: The ability to rapidly visualize a wide range of ideas significantly sped up the design process, allowing for more time to be spent on refinement and client interaction

- **Increased creativity and flexibility**: The Outlier Group was able to explore more creative and diverse design options, tailoring their proposals more closely to client needs and preferences

- **Enhanced client engagement**: The realistic and detailed visuals generated by DALL-E 3 improved client understanding and engagement, leading to more effective collaboration

Conclusion

DALL-E 3 provided The Outlier Group with a powerful tool for visualization, greatly enhancing their design and presentation capabilities in interior design, architecture, and urban planning. This case study demonstrates the potential of AI to transform the design industry, offering innovative solutions for visualizing and communicating complex design concepts.

Having explored the impactful case studies highlighting DALL-E 3's revolutionary role in various industries, we now transition to the interviews with the pioneers who are at the forefront of this technological integration.

Interviews

In this section, we will gain some valuable insights into the world of generative AI through conversations with experts in the field. These interviews will provide a firsthand look at the experiences, strategies, and visions of those at the forefront of AI development and implementation. Now, let's dive into our engaging conversations with the following esteemed individuals:

- Gene Bernardin, Founder of Anthea AI

- Rory Flynn, AdWorld Pro Speaker

- Luis Garcia, President of PETE Learning

An Interview with Gene Bernardin

Gene Bernardin is a Generative AI Evangelist and Founder of Anthea AI, an AI consulting business.

Anthea AI is dedicated to translating the complex promise of AI, with its vast and endless possibilities, into practical understanding, enabling businesses to create a vision for actionable strategies.

LinkedIn Profile: `https://www.linkedin.com/services/page/b143993241154875a5/`

Q. How do you see DALL-E 3 pushing the boundaries of creative expression, and what are some of the most surprising or innovative uses of this technology you've encountered?

A: First, let's consider the implications of DALL-E 3 as a creative tool for a minute. Where traditional artist's tools, such as the sculptor's chisel, the painter's paintbrush, or the photographer's camera, are vehicles for the artist's skill (the implementation of which requires natural talent and years of study to develop), DALL-E 3 is a vehicle for the user's imagination. This is the true democratization of creativity. Unencumbered by one's artistic limitations, one's imagination becomes the direct source of creative expression, free of any limitation save for its own. Of course, the artist's imagination has always been the key driver of artistic expression, but the realization of this expression has always been reliant upon the artistic skill of the person wielding it. No more. DALL-E 3 releases the imagination from the restrictive confines of the creator's artistic limits and allows for a more direct expression between the imagination and the resulting creation.

Additionally, DALL-E 3 does not simply release us from the shackles of artistic skill sets; the generative nature of diffusion models is as comfortable with fantasy as it is with reality and does not perceive the difference as we might. Because of that, it opens creative horizons and easily blends genres. The imagination has no real-world limitation, and because of that, DALL-E 3 can act as a true collaborator in the expression of that limitlessness.

This quality is one of the most boundary-pushing aspects of DALL-E 3, with its ability to synthesize and reinterpret ideas and blend styles and elements that might not naturally occur to an artist or user. This, in turn, leads to the creation of unique, often surreal artworks that can inspire and challenge our perceptions of art and creativity, and it can just as easily create realistic representations of the world around us.

And because DALL-E 3 works with GPT-4/Bing Chat/Copilot, it can iterate images on non-image-specific text prompts. I often feed my articles to GPT-4 and ask it to use DALL-E 3 to provide a visual representation of its contents for use as the article's banner or teaser image.

Some of the more surprising and innovative uses of DALL-E 3 involve using it to visualize complex ideas, compose scenes that would be impossible to capture in real life, design everything from clothing to architecture, and enhance storytelling in new mediums. For example, creators are using it to visualize intricate worlds and characters for graphic novels and video games. Architects are experimenting with generating design concepts that incorporate styles previously not combined. Photographers are even using it to create scenes and backdrops that would be too dangerous, expensive, or impractical to capture physically.

What's perhaps most exciting is that we're still just scratching the surface of what's possible. As DALL-E 3 and other diffusion models continue advancing and people dream up new creative applications, I expect the boundaries of artistic expression to be pushed exponentially further in terms of originality, complexity, realism, and more. We may see innovations emerge that combine mediums, such as animation, digital art, and photography, in unprecedented ways. With AI, the limits of imagination are boundless, so DALL-E 3 grants an amazing new dimension for creativity, unlike anything we've had access to before.

I'm eager to see how creators continue to unlock new creative frontiers. The future promises innovations in expression that we can only begin to imagine today.

Q. In your perspective, how can artists and creatives maintain their unique voice and style when working with AI tools such as DALL-E 3? What's the key to striking a balance between AI-generated content and human creativity?

A: Let's be clear: DALL-E 3, like all generative AI models, is a tool, and as such, it merely amplifies or augments the creativity of the user. Just as the paintbrush allows the artist to create art through the medium of painting, DALL-E 3 allows the artist to express themselves in a visual medium through a generative and iterative process by using words to express their creative intent. Language becomes the brushstrokes. The artist decides when the creation is representative of their artistic voice. They never lose that control. DALL-E 3 is merely a new tool. In that regard, works created with DALL-E 3 will always maintain the artist's unique voice and style.

Artists may fear that the removal of creative barriers will weaken their value (in one instance, I even had an artist insist that suffering was necessary to create art and, therefore, images created with artificial intelligence would never be art); however, I would argue that the creation of true art is the aesthetic inherent in the finished composition. This will always convey the artist's sensibilities and intent, regardless of how it was created.

I'd also like to point out that being able to create images (even interesting ones) does not make one an artist or the creation "art," just as owning a camera does not make one a professional photographer. Yes, indeed, taking a picture is easy, but creating a photograph to the standards of a professional photographer is not so much.

I can only imagine that when cameras were first introduced, artists wondered about their future when photographic images could be used instead of painted representations. And when digital cameras made photography easy and inexpensive, and photoshop made manipulation of those images possible, professional photographers certainly feared for their livelihood.

True art is never diminished by "less than;" rather, it always stands out in stark contrast.

I should also say that I've seen many creative artists and photographers welcome new technologies that expand their capabilities and remove the tedious and time-consuming parts of their creative process, which ultimately only serve to inhibit and dampen their creativity and volume of output.

So, "What's the key to striking a balance between AI-generated content and human creativity?" The question supposes a separation where none exists. AI-generated content is the product of human creativity.

Q. For someone just starting out with generative AI, what are the most common challenges they might face with a tool such as DALL-E 3, and what tips can you offer to help them navigate and overcome these hurdles effectively?

A: The most common challenges for someone just starting out with generative AI are the following:

- Understanding how to prompt correctly
- Getting consistent and repeatable results

DALL-E 3 is the simplest of the image-creating generative AI diffusion models. This is because GPT-4 acts as its frontend, allowing for natural language prompting rather than the more complicated prompt engineering required by **Midjourney** and **Stable Diffusion**, which are models that have a significantly steeper learning curve in both prompting and feature usage. So, DALL-E 3 is much more suited for the new inexperienced user right out of the box

Tips: One very helpful tip for new users is to think of GPT-4 as a person and prompt as if you were talking to an actual person. This approach should act as the framework for your interaction. Using natural language, explain the image you would like to create, just like you were describing it to another person. The process is the same and doesn't require any coding or specific prompt engineering. You wouldn't expect another person to know what you wanted unless you were explicit, and the same proves true here. The more information you can give the model about what you want specifically in the image, the more likely you are to get what you expect. At the same time, it is okay to be non-specific if you are open to more creative or unexpected results.

By way of explanation, GPT-4 was trained on natural language dialog. So, it is most responsive to this form of communication. It was the foundation of its training. Interestingly, GPT-4 has even been shown to perform statistically better when prompted with positive reinforcement, just as a human would.

> **Important note**
> Refer back to *Chapter 1* to review the basics of DALL-E 3.

And just like a human, GPT-4/DALL-E 3 remembers context throughout the session. This allows for iteration. This means you can tweak the resulting images just by asking the model to make changes rather than starting each request from scratch. For instance, you might ask for an image of a fashionable Japanese woman in a white hat, and upon seeing the result, you can change the image simply by adding, "Now change the hat color to powder blue." Here, DALL-E 3 will remember your prior request and simply change the hat color, understanding that the image will include a fashionable Japanese woman.

Consistency: All generative AI models are non-deterministic by nature. Because of this, their exact output is somewhat unpredictable and not completely controllable. **Diffusion models** create images through a learning process of adding and removing noise, a generative process that does not lend itself to reproducing the same image consistently or reliably. The model is generating/creating a response based on each new prompt and not searching for an existing image, as search engines do. But there are some ways in which you can influence some consistency into your results.

Three helpful tips on how to achieve some level of consistency with images created by DALL-E 3 would be the following:

- The use of grids
- The use of expanded prompts
- Iterations

Let's say you would like to create a consistent image with some variations. In this case, let's say that I would like to create an image of a fashionable Japanese woman with several different facial expressions. I can accomplish this by creating a prompt that requests that the same image subject be placed in a grid with variations in each grid. Prompt example: "I would like you to create an image grid with six sections. In each section should be displayed a photographic portrait of the same fashionable Japanese woman with a `different facial expression in each."` This prompt should return an image with six sections; each section will be the same woman with a different expression.

When entering prompts, GPT-4 will expand/expound on that prompt before feeding it to DALL-E 3. It does this for a number of reasons:

- To apply OpenAI's preferential guidelines in order to avoid bias

- To apply any appropriate filters (to protect against harmful images)

- To expand on an otherwise limited prompt request (i.e., expanding the details of an image prompt that might otherwise be too vague, giving DALL-E 3 more context for the creation of the image)

If you have the expanded prompt of the created image, you can recreate a very similar image in the future.

Obtaining the expanded GPT-4 prompt for a particular image is as easy as asking GPT-4 for this. You can make this request as part of your initial prompt (i.e., `"...and provide me with the full image prompt you use to create the image"`) after the image has been created (i.e., `"Please provide me with the full expanded prompt you used to create the previous image"`) or by clicking on the created image and selecting the information icon in the upper right corner in the expanded view. Having that expanded prompt will allow for the future creation of very similar images.

Additionally, GPT-4/DALL-E 3 lets you iterate your prompts during a session to refine the output to your liking. When doing this, the model will retain the same expanded image prompt throughout the iterative process and simply change it according to your updated instructions (until such time as you make an entirely new/different image request). Because of this, iterations retain consistency in the look of the resulting images.

My final tip to new users is a general one: try. True understanding only comes through actually using DALL-E 3. You really just have to roll your sleeves up and get in there. Play and experiment; there are no mistakes in the learning process, aside from not trying. Success and failure are both great teachers. So don't be shy or intimidated.

Key takeaways

In our interview, Gene Bernardin shared his expertise and insightful observations, providing valuable takeaways for both professionals and enthusiasts. This discussion highlighted Bernardin's significant contributions, offering you an opportunity to understand his impact:

- **Iteration**: Feed articles to GPT-4 and ask it to use DALL-E 3 to provide a visual representation of its contents for use as the article's banner or teaser image. Although the book has discussed iteration extensively, this specific application has not been addressed until now. Discover and enjoy this novel insight here!

- **Expanded prompt**: Ask DALL-E to provide the expanded prompt used to create the image (i.e., "...and provide me with the full image prompt you use to create the image"). That expanded prompt will allow for the future creation of a similar image.

- **Grids**: Create a consistent image with some variations. This is similar to what we learned in *Chapter 2* when using the contact sheet prompt under the *Creative film types* section.

An interview with Rory Flynn

Rory Flynn is a pioneer in AI training and consulting and an **Ad World** pro speaker.

Ad World is an online advertising conference and learning platform for marketers. It's considered the world's largest online advertising event, with over 20,000 attendees.

LinkedIn Profile: `https://www.linkedin.com/in/rory-flynn-ai/`

Q: In your perspective, how can artists and creatives maintain their unique voice and style when working with AI tools such as DALL-E 3? What's the key to striking a balance between AI-generated content and human creativity?

A: The true art is in the prompt. Now, we just have to be able to translate our thoughts into words. Tools such as DALL-E 3 are extremely literal and will listen to what you say. Sure, they may fill in the blanks when you leave things out, but they're extremely good at taking direction.

Why is it great for beginners? There is a low barrier to entry, and DALL-E 3 will help you build a vision, even if you don't have one.

Why is it great for experts? As mentioned, the tool is extremely literal. So, if you have a unique vision, DALL-E can be your execution partner. It will take your step-by-step directions to get to the end result.

So, to me, it starts with having a vision. If you have an endpoint in sight, ChatGPT/DALL-E can guide you through the process. I also believe this will ignite human creativity. Earlier, if you didn't have the skills or knowledge to use tools such as Adobe Photoshop or Illustrator, your ideas were just ideas. With the tools we have now, you can actually bring your thoughts to life, test them, and manipulate them without needing to be a full-time artist or designer. With that being said, artists and designers are the most prepared to use the tools out of the gate. They know what it takes to get from concept to finished product, and they have the technical skills, they understand the verbiage, and they know how to visually construct an image.

Key takeaways

In our conversation with Rory, we learned that with DALL-E, tasks that once required extensive expertise in programs such as Adobe Illustrator or Photoshop can now be accomplished without this, at least to some extent. It's not all-encompassing, but certain functionalities are within reach. Some of the key points are the following:

- **DALL-E 3's prompt coherence is top-notch**: DALL-E 3 will generate whatever you put into the prompt. For example, if you use the prompt "`One large purple dog, one small green dog, snuggling on a dog bed, with toys and bones on the floor`," you will (usually) receive exactly what you asked for. This is not the same with all other image generators.

- **ChatGPT can guide you**: Working within the ChatGPT window allows you to have conversations with your prompts. You can edit certain elements or have ChatGPT provide suggestions. It's a more intuitive way of prompting and easier for beginners.

An Interview with Luis Garcia

Luis Garcia is the President of PETE Learning.

PETE is an AI-powered learning platform with a mission to revolutionize how knowledge is crafted, shared, and absorbed.

LinkedIn Profile: `https://www.linkedin.com/in/luisegarcia/`

Q: How do you envision the evolution of generative AI over the next decade, and what impact do you think it will have on various industries, including art, design, and entertainment?

A: I believe generative AI represents an inflection point in terms of the impact of technology on business and everyday life. In fact, I don't think we can fully understand the impact yet, but there are certain aspects we can see. It is obvious that it increases the output of content, with entertainment content included. Generative AI will be a bridge for those with imagination and no access to tools for visual creation. For example, someone can now come up with a story, write a script with ChatGPT, generate it, and refine the look of the characters, scenery, and shots with DALL-E, as well as generate a short video of the whole thing in Stable Diffusion. In a world where so much of the current entertainment is recycled, I'm excited about the future of new stories that we will get from new creative talent.

Q. How do you see generative AI tools, such as DALL-E 3, transforming everyday creative tasks for non-professionals, and what advice would you give to those looking to incorporate AI into their personal creative projects?

A: I'll give you a couple of examples. I used DALL-E 3 to create visuals for a sales presentation. We know that "a picture is worth 1,000 words," so I can make great visual presentations that convey my message using DALL-E. I am also using it to create unique visuals for social media posts. I can create something representing the brand and celebrate a holiday in seconds. Both tasks do not represent a big part of my day-to-day job, but I can do them without seeking professional assistance.

Key takeaways

In our conversation with Luis, we learned how DALL-E fits into business and everyday tasks. Let's look at a few takeaways:

- You can craft a script in ChatGPT and utilize DALL-E 3 to create characters, settings, and scenes. Then, you can bring the entire concept to life by producing a short video using Stable Diffusion.

- DALL-E 3 facilitates the quick and easy creation of unique visuals for social media posts, allowing for the representation of the brand without requiring professional graphic design skills and streamlining content creation for branding purposes.

- The use of DALL-E 3 enables the creation of impactful visuals for sales presentations, leveraging the adage "a picture is worth 1,000 words" to convey complex messages succinctly and effectively.

Summary

With this, we have finished the final chapter of this book. In this chapter, we looked at the diverse range of use cases, case studies, and insightful interviews with experts in the field of generative AI. This chapter serves as a cohesive synthesis of the various insights and findings, drawing together the conclusions from the practical applications and expert viewpoints we have explored.

I really hope you had as much fun reading this book as we had while creating it. It's been a journey packed with cool stuff, and I'm super excited for you to try out all the different styles we played around with in *Chapter 2*. Don't forget to give those templates in *Chapter 8* a whirl; they're there to make your life easier and more fun.

If you find yourself with questions about any of the content in the book, or if you simply wish to share your experiences and insights as you apply what you've learned, please feel free to connect with me on LinkedIn here: `https://www.linkedin.com/in/holly-picano-481a872/`.

I am always eager to engage in discussions, answer queries, and learn about how you are bringing the ideas from our book into your personal and professional endeavors. Your thoughts and experiences are invaluable, and I look forward to the opportunity to connect with fellow artistic and imaginative minds!

Index

U

V

packtpub.com

Subscribe to our online digital library for full access to over 7,000 books and videos, as well as industry leading tools to help you plan your personal development and advance your career. For more information, please visit our website.

Why subscribe?

- Spend less time learning and more time coding with practical eBooks and Videos from over 4,000 industry professionals
- Improve your learning with Skill Plans built especially for you
- Get a free eBook or video every month
- Fully searchable for easy access to vital information
- Copy and paste, print, and bookmark content

Did you know that Packt offers eBook versions of every book published, with PDF and ePub files available? You can upgrade to the eBook version at packtpub.com and as a print book customer, you are entitled to a discount on the eBook copy. Get in touch with us at customercare@packtpub.com for more details.

At www.packtpub.com, you can also read a collection of free technical articles, sign up for a range of free newsletters, and receive exclusive discounts and offers on Packt books and eBooks.

Other Books You May Enjoy

If you enjoyed this book, you may be interested in these other books by Packt:

Unlocking the Secrets of Prompt Engineering

Gilbert Mizrahi

ISBN: 978-1-83508-383-3

- Explore the different types of prompts, their strengths, and weaknesses
- Understand the AI agent's knowledge and mental model
- Enhance your creative writing with AI insights for fiction and poetry
- Develop advanced skills in AI chatbot creation and deployment
- Discover how AI will transform industries such as education, legal, and others
- Integrate LLMs with various tools to boost productivity
- Understand AI ethics and best practices, and navigate limitations effectively
- Experiment and optimize AI techniques for best results

The Future of Finance with ChatGPT and Power BI

James Bryant, Aloke Mukherjee

ISBN: 978-1-80512-334-7

- Dominate investing, trading, and reporting with ChatGPT's game-changing insights
- Master Power BI for dynamic financial visuals, custom dashboards, and impactful charts
- Apply AI and ChatGPT for advanced finance analysis and natural language processing (NLP) in news analysis
- Tap into ChatGPT for powerful market sentiment analysis to seize investment opportunities
- Unleash your financial analysis potential with data modeling, source connections, and Power BI integration
- Understand the importance of data security and adopt best practices for using ChatGPT and Power BI

Packt is searching for authors like you

If you're interested in becoming an author for Packt, please visit authors.packtpub.com and apply today. We have worked with thousands of developers and tech professionals, just like you, to help them share their insight with the global tech community. You can make a general application, apply for a specific hot topic that we are recruiting an author for, or submit your own idea.

Share Your Thoughts

Now you've finished *Generating Creative Images With DALL-E 3*, we'd love to hear your thoughts! Scan the QR code below to go straight to the Amazon review page for this book and share your feedback or leave a review on the site that you purchased it from.

https://packt.link/r/1-835-08771-X

Your review is important to us and the tech community and will help us make sure we're delivering excellent quality content.

Download a free PDF copy of this book

Thanks for purchasing this book!

Do you like to read on the go but are unable to carry your print books everywhere?

Is your eBook purchase not compatible with the device of your choice?

Don't worry, now with every Packt book you get a DRM-free PDF version of that book at no cost.

Read anywhere, any place, on any device. Search, copy, and paste code from your favorite technical books directly into your application.

The perks don't stop there, you can get exclusive access to discounts, newsletters, and great free content in your inbox daily

Follow these simple steps to get the benefits:

1. Scan the QR code or visit the link below

https://packt.link/free-ebook/9781835087718

2. Submit your proof of purchase
3. That's it! We'll send your free PDF and other benefits to your email directly